Leadership Skills
for
Managers, Supervisors and Team Leaders

by
Louis E. Tagliaferri

New 2010 edition is based on the author's previous work titled The Total Quality Leader published by Talico Inc. 1987 and revised 2002.

Talico Developmental Systems L.C.
4304 Blue Heron Dr.
Ponte Vedra Beach, FL 32082
www.talico.com
Copyright 2011 Louis E. Tagliaferri

Copyright Notice

This book and all contents herein is the copyrighted work of the author and the proprietary product of both the author and of Talico Developmental Systems L.C. Copying or reproduction in any form by any means without the express written permission of the author is strictly prohibited.

Table of Contents

	Introduction	Page	iii
1.	The Role And Responsibility Of A Leader	Page	1
2.	Developing Leadership Skills	Page	11
3.	Building A Winning Team	Page	21
4.	Communicating And Active Listening	Page	31
5.	Motivating Through Empowerment	Page	43
6.	Solving Problems Effectively	Page	51
7.	Improving Planning Skills	Page	61
8.	Training Employees To Succeed	Page	71
9.	Improving Employee Work Performance	Page	81
10.	Coaching And Counseling	Page	91
11.	Cultural Diversity	Page	103
12.	Total Quality Leadership	Page	113
	Appendix A – Self-Awareness Test Answers	Page	123
	Appendix B – Dr. W. Edward Deming's 14 Points	Page	137
	Appendix C – Leadership Skills Test	Page	139
	References	Page	151

Introduction

The nature of the role that most managers and supervisors are required to fulfill requires that they accomplish things through others; in other words, their role requires that they be leaders. Unfortunately, the majority of managers and supervisors in business, industry, government and other organizational sectors were appointed to their current positions mainly because of their technical skill - not because of their leadership ability. It is true that some people are "born" leaders, but the majority are not. Therefore, if a person is to succeed as a manager, supervisor or other organizational leader, he or she must acquire leadership skills through training and experience.

The purpose of this book is to provide managers, supervisors, other organizational leaders and candidates for these positions with the fundamental knowledge and skill development that they need to succeed as leaders in today's business environment. The book consists of twelve chapters that focus on essential leadership skills. Each chapter clearly sets forth chapter learning objectives. Instructional text follows punctuated by a series of Key Points that highlight crucial leadership learning issues.

At the end of each chapter the reader is presented with a Self-Awareness Test that will provide feedback regarding how well he or she understands the leadership issues and principles presented. (Answers to the test items will be found in Appendix B). Concluding each chapter is a structured format by which the reader can prepare a Personal Developmental Plan that will help him or her gain introspection about developmental needs related to the topic of the chapter and then prepare developmental goals and a set of strategies by which the goals can be accomplished.

A final and most valuable feature of the book is the Leadership Skills Test that will be found in Appendix C. This 40 paired-item test measures the extent that the respondent's leadership beliefs and behaviors are congruent with those that research has found are characteristic of the most successful leaders.

The concepts and principles presented in this book are based on extensive research as well as on the author's personal experience as a business executive and management consultant that spans over 40 years. Learn them well. Most are timeless and will surely serve you well in your career as an organizational leader.

Chapter One
The Role And Responsibility Of A Leader

> ## Learning Objectives
> After completing this chapter you will have learned:
>
> The role of a leader.
>
> The responsibilities that a leader has toward his or her employees, peers and superiors.
>
> The essential skills and functions required of leaders.

One of the most difficult tasks for someone in a supervisory position is to clearly define his or her role as a leader. What is a leader? How does the job of a leader differ from that of other employees? What are the major functions and components of a leader's job? If you are a leader in your organization, a manager, supervisor or other work group leader, it is important that you understand the answers to these questions.

Key Point
The role of a leader is to influence people and to accomplish things through others.

The role of a leader is to influence people and to accomplish things through others. Accomplishing things through others is a role that is very difficult for many people, especially for newly appointed leaders. For example, some people who currently hold a position as a manager or supervisor were previously non-supervisory employees in either another organization or in their current organization - perhaps, even in the same work group that they now supervise. This means that in the past they may have personally performed the same kind of work that is being performed by the employees that they now supervise. Now, instead of producing a product or performing a service themselves, as a leader they must accomplish these tasks through others.

Even if you are a "working supervisor" and spend part of your time doing the same work as your employees, you still must accomplish the majority of your work group's overall task through others. This is the major difference between the job of a supervisor and that of non-supervisory employees -- accomplishing work through others. However, particularly when it is necessary to meet a deadline or a production quota, many newly appointed supervisors who have been promoted from within the organization ("from the ranks") find it very difficult to refrain from "jumping in" and working right next to their subordinates doing the same work as they do. There is nothing wrong with performing a task or work operation for purposes of training employees and demonstrating proper methods or procedures. But, the principal job of supervisors is to supervise – not performing line work.

Another difference between managers, supervisors and other work group leaders is the scope of their responsibilities. Non-supervisory employees are usually responsible only for themselves. However, as a leader you also have responsibilities toward several other groups of people including those employees whom you supervise, your peers and your superiors. Let us briefly examine these responsibilities.

Key Point
Leaders have responsibilities to the employees they supervise, to their peers and to their superiors.

First, consider the responsibilities that you, as a supervisor or leader, have toward your employees. The most important of these responsibilities are:

1. Treating employees as you, yourself, would want to be treated. This means, first and foremost, respecting the employee's personal dignity, being courteous, friendly, fair and respectful.

2. Making sure that employees fully understand what you expect of them and how well they are doing. This includes introducing or orientating new employees to their work areas, fellow employees, their jobs, and company policy and work rules. It also covers on-the-job training, skill development, setting performance standards and letting employees know how well they are meeting those standards.

3. Being a coach, helper, listener and problem solver. Perhaps the most critical is being a listener because effective listening affects all of the other functions.

4. Creating a work environment in which, to the extent possible, employees find job satisfaction. This also includes ensuring that the work conditions are safe, healthy and at least reasonably pleasant. It also means ensuring that employees' motivational needs are being met as fully as practicable.

Your responsibilities toward your peers are equally important. Leaders frequently interact with employees at their own level, either within their department or elsewhere within the organization. For example, whether your work group performs a service or produces a component or product, it will require inputs from others outside the immediate work group. In turn, your work group provides outputs to others (internal customers). This affects your peers in other work groups.

Key Point
As a leader you have an important responsibility to work collaboratively with your peers in other work groups. Teamwork can produce outstanding results!

Among the key responsibilities you have toward your peers are:

1. Being cooperative, friendly and courteous. Teamwork both within your own work group and between you and your fellow supervisors can produce

outstanding results. But, it depends on how well you cooperate with others and on the quality of your interpersonal relationships.

2. Being open, candid and honest in your communications. This relates to cooperation and is an obvious "must" within your own work group). Because of work group interdependency, trust and communication must be of the highest levels.

3. Working with peers collaboratively toward a common goal. Territorial attitudes are inappropriate. You all work for the same organization. If one department or work group suffers because of lack of cooperation and teamwork, then the entire organization suffers.

Key Point
Most leaders are part of the management team. Therefore, a key responsibility of leaders is to support management policy and decisions.

You also have a responsibility toward your superiors and to your organization:

1. Representing management's point of view. Because you are part of your organization's management team, you have an important responsibility to support management policy and decisions. As a leader you represent management in your dealings with employees. Failure to do this is one of the more serious lapses of responsibility that a supervisor can have.

2. Taking proper care of machinery, equipment, facilities, material and other physical assets. This means ensuring that proper preventative maintenance schedules are followed, using material resources efficiently, protecting the environment and promoting proper safety and health conditions.

3. Focusing on total quality performance. This includes having a high degree of cost, quality and productivity consciousness, being dedicated to meeting all of your internal and external customers' needs and expectations, striving for continuous improvement and meeting schedules and deadlines.

Key Point
All managers, supervisors and other work group leaders must have three types of skill: technical, human and conceptual.

There are three types of skills that any leader needs in order to be effective and to fulfill his or her responsibilities toward subordinates, peers and superiors; these are technical, conceptual and human skills. Technical skills are those skills relating to job knowledge and to the technical nature of the job. A supervisor of nurses must understand the medical technology related to that profession and most are also licensed nursing practitioners. A production supervisor must understand assembly, fabrication and similar factory operations. A supervisor of accounting must have technical skill in cost accounting, accounts receivables, payables, payroll and similar functions.

Another skill is conceptual skill. This is the skill leaders need to anticipate a future event and develop strategies to deal with it. It also is the skill of thinking in abstract terms and of being innovative and creative. Finally, there are the human skills. These are the skills which are required to interact effectively with fellow employees. They are also called interpersonal or interaction skills.

Leaders require all of these skills. However, experience has shown that the problem solving and employee contact nature of a first-level supervisor's job requires a greater amount of technical and human skills. On the other hand, conceptual skills are especially important for top management executives who are an organization's primary visionaries and who engage in a lot of long range planning.

Key Point
The functions of planning, organizing, directing and controlling are called the "Management Cycle."

Human, technical and conceptual skills are applied within what is called the Management Cycle that consists of the functions of Planning, Organizing, Directing and Controlling. This is also known as the Supervisory Process.

> *Planning*: Setting objectives and developing strategies to accomplish the objectives, i.e. developing a plan.

Organizing: Gathering together the manpower, monetary and material resources needed to put the plan into effect.

Directing: Staffing, training, making work assignments, coaching, problem solving, communicating and other behaviors required to put the plan into effect.

Controlling: Making sure that the plan is working as designed and taking corrective action when it is not; e.g., problem solving, performance coaching or administering discipline.

Summary

Your role as a manager, supervisor or other work group leader is an especially important one. Your personal attitude, behavior and leadership practices have a crucial direct impact on the employees of your work group and of other work groups as well -- for better or for worse. In order for you personally to function effectively as a leader you must clearly understand that leaders accomplish work through others. As leaders influence others to accomplish tasks, they have responsibilities toward the employees they supervise, to their peers and to their superiors. These responsibilities include treating all employees fairly, making sure that employees have sufficient, timely and accurate job related information, motivating them to succeed and providing them with the resources they need to get their jobs done properly.

Leaders also have a responsibility to work effectively with their peers and to effectively use and maintain the equipment, tools, supplies and other resources provided by their employer. In the discharge of these responsibilities, managers, supervisors and other work group leaders must use technical, conceptual and human skills. They also must have skill using all four functions of the Management Cycle: Planning, Organizing, Directing, and Controlling.

The Role And Responsibility Of A Leader Self-Awareness Test

Instructions: Decide whether each of the statements below is true **(T)**, false **(F)** or whether you are uncertain **(?)** about it. Indicate your decision by placing a mark in the appropriate column to the right of each statement.

		T	?	F
01.	A major difference between the role of a leader and other employees is that leaders accomplish things primarily through others.	☐	☐	☐
02.	The true mark of a manager, supervisor or other leader is the extent that he or she can successfully compete against peers in other work groups.	☐	☐	☐
03.	The main responsibility of managers, supervisors and other leaders is to represent the best interests of the employees they supervise.	☐	☐	☐
04.	The most important skill a supervisor must have is conceptual skill, the ability to forecast and plan.	☐	☐	☐
05.	Working supervisors require less human and conceptual skill than other supervisors.	☐	☐	☐
06.	The term "Management Cycle" refers to the career path that most leaders progress through during their work lives.	☐	☐	☐
07.	Objectives setting is part of the planning function.	☐	☐	☐
08.	True leaders direct subordinates' activities rather than simply influence them to do things.	☐	☐	☐
09.	Making sure that a plan is carried out as designed should be the responsibility of an organization's planning department.	☐	☐	☐
10.	Training, communicating and making work assignments are part of the directing function.	☐	☐	☐

Personal Developmental Plan

Prepare a development plan to improve your knowledge and understanding about the leadership role that you are assigned in your organization:

A. The following is a description of the leadership role that I am currently assigned:

B. Included in the above leadership role are the following major responsibilities that I have toward my subordinates, peers and superiors:

C. In order to understand my leadership role and responsibilities better I need the following additional information:

D. Specific strategies for developing and strengthening my understanding about my leadership role and responsibilities are:

Chapter 2
Developing Leadership Skills

Learning Objectives

After completing this chapter you will have learned:

The functions, characteristics and styles of leadership.

How to assess your own leadership style and effectiveness.

How to determine which leadership style is most effective in any particular situation.

Recently, an information technology company decided to conduct a training program for its supervisors and managers. Meetings were held with all management employees to announce the program. During the meetings, the company human resources manager emphasized that the main reason the company was conducting the program was to strengthen the organization's leadership. She pointed out that leadership development was especially important at a time when the company was experiencing economic difficulties due to domestic and foreign competition, because effective leadership was crucial to the vitality and survivability of the company.

In the case above, the human resources manager was absolutely correct. No organization can afford to have weak leadership. However, exactly what is leadership and how does it work? Leadership exists whenever one person agrees to follow the direction of another person. But, anyone who has held leadership responsibilities knows that it is not that simple. In fact, leadership involves a complex set of relationships and interdependencies. It is an integral part of the art and practice of managing and supervising and in the final analysis, it depends entirely on the willingness of a follower to accept leadership from a leader. In other words, no matter how hard a leader tries to lead or what leadership styles he or she might use, there will be no leadership without follower acceptance.

Key Point
The basis of leadership is power of influence like reward, tradition, charisma, expertise and rational agreement.

The basis for leadership is a power or influence. There are five major powers or influences which most leaders can exercise in order to secure acceptance by followers:

1. **The Power of Fear, Punishment and Reward**

    This is "power" in the literal sense. On the basis of appointed, elected or assumed position authority, some leaders lead by using the "carrot or stick" approach. In this case, followers usually are rewarded when they satisfactorily comply with the leader's instructions and are punished when they do not. Thus, the specific power or influence is fear. Followers fear the consequences of failing to comply with the leader's instructions and/or fear the loss of a reward if they do not.

2. **The Power of Tradition**

    Custom and tradition are strong influences. It is customary and traditional for employees to follow the instructions of their supervisors and to accept the leadership of people who are formally appointed to positions of authority. Almost every type of organization, from the military to business to the church, has a hierarchy of leadership that is traditionally based, in large part, upon appointed or elected authority.

3. **The Power of Charisma**

   Sometimes leaders lead (for better or worse) partly because they have a dynamic, charismatic personality. It almost is as though there was a magnetism attracting people to follow the leadership of certain people. Historical examples of this are Caesar, Alexander the Great, Christ, Gandhi, Hitler, Kennedy and many others.

4. **The Power of Expertise**

   From time to time each of us agrees to follow the leadership of someone else on the basis of their expertise. When we are ill we readily follow the advice (leadership) of a doctor and for legal matters we follow the advice of an attorney. Consultants lead by power of expertise. We follow the leadership of trade people, such as plumbers or electricians, when their help is needed. In a business organization people follow the expert leadership of technical and staff specialists.

5. **The Power of Rational Agreement**

   Another reason why people follow leaders is because they know, understand and accept that the particular instruction or direction being given by a leader is the correct thing to do in that situation. The leader (or, in some cases, the circumstances themselves) has sufficiently explained the situation so that reasonable people can rationally accept the leader's decision and take the desired course of action.

Key Point
The power of rational agreement is very effective with today's culturally diverse and empowered work force.

Obviously, leadership is not that simple. Sometimes several powers or influences are in use at the same time. A charismatic person might also have a great deal of expertise in a certain area. Some leaders may sequence their use of powers of influence while others adapt themselves to the particulars of the situation that requires the exercise of leadership behavior. In today's rapidly changing and culturally diverse work force many leaders are finding considerable success using the power of rational agreement, especially with respect to programs involving team building and employee empowerment.

The above powers of influence help to explain why people follow leaders. They do not explain why some leaders are more successful than others. During the past several years a number of studies have been conducted to identify the characteristics that distinguish superior leaders from those who are less successful. Essentially, superior leaders refuse to settle for mediocrity. They continually strive to achieve excellence in their own jobs and they motivate and coach their subordinates to attain the same goals.

Key Point
Superior leaders refuse to settle for mediocrity. They continually strive to achieve performance excellence.

In addition, superior leaders share these important leadership qualities:

Pride & Confidence -- Superior leaders feel good about both their personal conduct and about their personal work behavior. They are confident about their skills and abilities. They take pride in the quality and effectiveness of their job performance and they are proud of their subordinates and the work they perform.

Work Ethic -- Superior leaders have a strong, positive work ethic. They work hard, applying themselves diligently and effectively to their assigned jobs. They expect the same attitude and behavior from their subordinates.

Work Standards -- Superior leaders are true craftspeople. They set high, yet attainable, standards of conduct and performance for themselves and for their subordinates. They expect and achieve quality and excellence.

Teamwork -- Superior leaders are team players. They participate in and involve others in developing new ideas, planning and problem solving. They openly share job related information with others and empower their employees through the principle of shared responsibility.

Values -- Superior leaders recognize and respect the value and worth of the individual. They treat others, whether subordinates, peers or superiors, as they want to be treated themselves. Their core value system of personal, family, spiritual and career values are examples and models that inspire others.

Creativity -- Superior leaders are creative and innovative and they encourage the same from their subordinates. They find ways to overcome barriers that stop others and as a result they succeed when others fail.

Leadership -- Superior leaders accomplish things through others by focusing people on a vision, helping them develop new competencies and by helping people overcome obstacles, failure and disappointment. They lead by example, rather than rely on power, and they include their empowered subordinates in their success.

Key Point
The five basic leadership styles are directive, persuasive, consultative, participative and delegative.

There are five basic styles or approaches that leaders can use in the exercise of the powers of influence that demonstrate the above leadership qualities and characteristics:

1. **Directive** - This is an autocratic style of leadership. When using this style, the leader relies heavily on one-way, downward communication with followers. He or she "tells" the employee precisely what to do, when and how to do it, where it should be done and all other details of the task.

    This is a "cards on the table" approach is sometimes needed with non-responsive followers. A directive style is also often required when dealing with new, inexperienced employees. However, a directive leadership style tends to block upward communication and does not encourage people to be creative or innovative.

2. **Persuasive** - When using a persuasive or "selling" leadership style a leader still is quite directive. Now, though, he or she takes the time to explain why the instruction is "best" and to answer questions. This style shares many of the advantages and disadvantages of a directive style. However, it can obtain greater cooperation from employees, as long as it is not perceived to be manipulative.

3. **Consultative** - Consultative leaders are willing to sincerely obtain input from followers <u>before</u> making a final decision. The leader usually will state the issue or problem and ask followers for their opinions or suggestions. After listening to the inputs, the leader then decides and acts; often modifying his or her decision based upon follower input.
This leadership approach provides far better follower involvement and leads to greater acceptance of the leader's final decision. It also improves decision accuracy. It is reasonably easy and efficient to use and it facilitates improved two-way communication.

4. **Participative** – With this leadership style the leader actually gives up part of his or her decision making power. The leader invites employees to fully participate in the decision making process and together with them reaches a consensus decision. Leadership is through the power of rational agreement. This leadership style is excellent for obtaining commitment to goals and objectives. However, a participative approach can be very slow and time consuming and requires considerable leader skill. A participative approach can also lead to work group frustration - especially if consensus is not achieved and the leader reverts to a more directive oriented style.

5. **Delegative** - In this style, the leader turns over (delegates) the entire matter to the followers for their decision. He or she is mainly interested in results rather than about how the results are attained. A delegative leadership approach is quick and easy to use. It is relatively efficient since leader's time is kept free. Further, delegation facilitates follower growth and development.

   At the same time delegation can be risky. In order to ensure that the desired results are attained followers must be fully competent in the delegated task and must be mature, responsible employees. Interestingly, a delegative approach does not foster improved human relations or communications since contact between leader and followers is at "arms length."

Key Point
There is no one best style of leadership. Rather, the most appropriate style depends on several situational variables.

Which leadership style a leader should use depends on the nature of the job or task to be done, the experience, training, skill and responsibility of his or her employees, and certain circumstances, such as time, cost, precedent, etc. This is called "situational leadership". It is based upon the premise that there is no one best way to lead all of the time. Rather, the most effective leader is one who adapts his or her leadership style to the variables just discussed.

Here is how to determine which leadership style you should use in various situations. First, determine the extent to which your subordinates have the experience, training, skill, willingness and responsibility to do the job or task which you have assigned them. This is called their job maturity. Rate them as having **High, Moderately High, Moderate, Moderately Low or Low** job maturity. The maturity of a worker will change with experience, training and growth. Because of this you should frequently reassess your maturity rating of each employee. Use the scale below as a guide to help you match your leadership style with the job maturity of the employees who you supervise.

Leadership Maturity Scale

Maturity Rating	Leadership Style
- Low	- Directive
- Moderately Low	- Persuasive
- Moderate	- Consultative
- Moderately High	- Participative
- High	- Delegative

Summary

Leadership is a critical skill and practice that directly affects the strength and vitality of any organization. Effective leadership is a lot more than just telling someone what to do or how to do it. A leader can lead only if followers accept and willingly follow his or her leadership. There are five powers or influences by which leaders secure follower acceptance. These are the powers of:

- Fear, Punishment and Reward
- Tradition
- Charisma
- Expertise
- Rational Agreement

Of these, only the power of rational agreement secures true, long-term commitment and follower acceptance.

Superior leaders can be distinguished from those who are less successful by their refusal to settle for mediocrity and by their determination to strive for performance excellence, both for themselves and for their subordinates. In addition, superior leaders share other qualities and characteristics like pride and self-confidence, a positive work ethic, high work standards, a value for individual worth and dignity, and the ability to be creative and innovative. They also lead people to accomplish things by helping them to focus on a vision and by helping them to grow and develop new competencies.

Studies have shown that there is no one best leadership style or approach for all situations. Rather, the best way to lead depends on several variables, such as the job, people and other circumstances. There are five major styles of leadership that can be adapted to these situations: directive, persuasive, consultative, participative and delegative. Your ability to diagnose a situation that requires leadership behavior and your flexibility, adaptability and facility with alternative leadership styles directly affects your overall leadership effectiveness.

Developing Leadership Skills Self-Awareness Test

Instructions: Decide whether each of the statements below is true **(T)**, false **(F)** or whether you are uncertain **(?)** about it. Indicate your decision by placing a mark in the appropriate column to the right of each statement.

		T	?	F
01.	Leaders can be effective even when followers do not accept their leadership.	☐	☐	☐
02.	Effective leadership is based on delegated power.	☐	☐	☐
03.	Participative Management is the most effective leadership style.	☐	☐	☐
04.	Employee empowerment reduces leadership power.	☐	☐	☐
05.	The power of rational agreement is usually best for obtaining follower commitment to work group goals.	☐	☐	☐
06.	A persuasive or selling style of leadership still involves the leader using a directive approach.	☐	☐	☐
07.	It can be fairly time consuming to use a consultative or participative style of leadership.	☐	☐	☐
08.	The best leadership style depends on variables like the people, the task and the situation.	☐	☐	☐
09.	Delegative leaders are more concerned about results than about how the results are achieved.	☐	☐	☐
10.	Effective leaders focus on achieving total quality performance through teamwork, empowerment and continuous improvement.	☐	☐	☐

Personal Developmental Plan

Prepare a development plan to improve your leadership skills by answering the following questions:

A.   The leadership skills that I use most frequently and that are currently my greatest strengths are:

B.   The leadership skills in which I currently need the greatest improvement are:

C.   My personal objectives for improving my use of leadership skills are:

D.   The specific strategies by which I plan to develop and strengthen my leadership skills ability are (use additional paper if necessary):

       1.

       2.

       3.

       4.

       5.

Chapter 3
Building A Winning Team

> ## Learning Objectives
>
> **After completing this chapter you will have learned:**
>
> What groups are and how groups function.
>
> What the difference is between a group and a team.
>
> What must be done in order to develop a winning team in your work group.

The most successful managers, supervisors and other work group leaders understand the nature of group dynamics and use this knowledge to transform the employees in their work groups into a winning team.

Key Point
The most successful managers, supervisors and other work group leaders transform their employees into a winning team.

Psychologists have found that most people have strong social and affiliation needs. Because of this it is inevitable that groups of people form and that most people affiliate with groups. Groups will be found everywhere in our society. People affiliate with churches, civic and fraternal organizations, community action groups, political organizations, hobby clubs, sports organizations, youth groups and every other imaginable type of group. At work the organization as a whole can be considered a group. However, within the organization are many different types of subgroups like departments, work stations, assembly lines, committees and task teams. Because groups are so much a part of our lives it is unlikely that you can think of anyone you know personally who is not a member of a group.

Key Point
All groups have distinguishing characteristics like a common purpose, common attitudes, unity, social control and structure.

Groups are made up of people who possess individual characteristics and traits. However, a group can often takes on characteristics which are quite different from those of the individuals within the group. Here are some of the distinguishing characteristics of groups:

1. *Common Purpose:* People tend to form groups when there is a common purpose or objective to be accomplished. An example would be a citizens' action group forming to help protect a neighborhood through a "crime watch" program.

2. *Common Attitudes:* Members within a group often share a common outlook or have similar interests and values.

3. *Unity:* Groups can often accomplish far more that individual members can by virtue of the strength, unity and cohesiveness of their combined effort.

4. *Social Control:* Groups develop their own codes or norms of social behavior. They establish a broad range of standards from job performance standards and work quotas to rules governing conduct, customs and ritual.

5. *Structure:* Eventually, groups develop their own hierarchy by establishing rank and status within the group.

Another interesting characteristic of groups is that they can be either formal or informal. Formal groups are usually appointed, elected or formed through consensus (acclamation). Examples of formal groups in business are quality improvement teams, formal work units, budget review committees, safety committees and company credit unions. Formal groups usually have leaders who have been appointed or elected.

Informal groups may take the form of subgroups within formal groups, e.g. a small group of employees who always sit together at lunch and play cards or a small group of employees who resist the introduction of new or improved work methods.

Informal groups usually have leaders, also. However, leadership of informal groups is rarely elected or appointed; instead it simply evolves. It is very important to note that for better or worse, informal groups and informal group leaders can often have more influence on employee behavior than formal groups and formal group leaders.

Key Point
Informal groups and informal group leaders can often have more influence on employee behavior than formal groups.

Groups are not necessarily teams. In fact, there can be a very considerable difference between a team and a group, even though groups and teams share certain of the same characteristics. Within both groups and teams there can be found the elements of common purposes, common attitudes, unity, social control and structure. However, in order for a group to be a team there must be something more. Members of a team not only have a common purpose but in addition they are mutually committed to achieve a common goal. They fully share information that is relevant about their task or mission with each other in an open, honest and candid way. All of the members of a team actively participate in the team's problem solving efforts to the full extent of their individual and collective capabilities.

Key Point
Members of a team are mutually committed to achieve a common goal. They actively participate in performing the team's task to the best of their capabilities.

Team members encourage one another and try to tap the full creative potential of all team members. They have a special sense of team loyalty and cohesiveness. When disagreement or conflict arises they deal with it openly and constructively using problem solving rather than trying to suppress it or compromise. And, team members share responsibility as well as rewards or recognition for their accomplishments. On the surface you might think that this description also fits practically any group. But this is not the case. For example, a group is still a group if there is unresolved conflict among group members or if some group members withhold relevant problem solving information from the others. But if this occurs the group is most definitely not a team. The importance of this difference is that teams are capable of doing something that is impossible for most groups. While it is true that the product of a group can be superior to the product of the average individuals within the group, teams can achieve synergism! Synergism occurs when the product of the team is superior to the product of the best, not average, individual on the team. In other words, in teams two plus two can equal more than four!

Key Point
Synergism occurs when the product of a team is superior to the product of the best individual on the team.

It is possible for teams to be leaderless. Some organizations are experimenting with what is termed "self-directed teams." These teams often do not have a formally appointed leader. Rather, each member of the team assumes responsibility for providing his or her share of team leadership as the situation requires. In fact, on any effective team leadership flows among the team members depending on any of several variables. Although self-directed and leaderless teams can serve a useful purpose under certain conditions, experience has proved that winning teams function most effectively if there is a formally appointed team leader.

The team leader on a winning team has a special role to perform that may be very different from his or her regularly assigned role within the organization -- especially if the team leader also holds a supervisory position. The appointment of a formal team leader does not relieve the team from sharing responsibility. This means that much of the responsibility for ensuring that the team productively focuses on the problem or task and at the same time maintain effective intra-team interaction is shared by all of the team members. This helps ensure the quality of the team's problem solving effort and at the same time provides a sense of shared satisfaction for the team's accomplishments among all team members.

Key Point
A winning team leader is a coach and a facilitator who shares power, responsibility and recognition with his or her employees.

A winning team leader is a coach and a facilitator. He or she leads through a process of influence that is significantly affected by the extent to which he or she is trusted and accepted by the other members of the team. While trust and acceptance is always important to a leader it is especially important when a leader is not the administrative superior of the team members. Further, the winning team leader shares power, responsibility and recognition for accomplishing the team's objectives with the other members of the team.

In one way, being a winning team leader is similar to being the leader of a voluntary community action group. The latter has very little position power and must influence group members in other ways. The members of a volunteer group can choose to follow or not follow the group leader; something that a subordinate of a supervisor is not free to do. Because the volunteer group leader cannot order or compel members to comply with directions or instructions he or she must find other ways to influence them.

Winning team members actively participate in their work group's activities because they are interested in the nature of their assignment and because they are committed to help accomplish the work group's objectives. They follow the leadership of their team leader not because they are compelled to but rather because they accept that person in a team leadership role.

Key Point
Winning team leaders engage in a set of behaviors that create an empowered work force.

At the same time, winning team leaders sustain their acceptance by their team members by engaging in a set of behaviors that combines a focus on the accomplishment of their goals with a focus on the needs and goals of the members of the team. They engage in a set of behaviors that create an empowered work force.

The late Dr. Dennis Kinlaw, an expert in superior team development, has found that the most successful team leaders regularly engage in team building practices that focus on:

1. **Action**: The team leader helps the team to get things done, solve problems and overcome organizational obstacles.

2. **Performance**: The team leader is a coach and a facilitator who strives for performance excellence on behalf of the team.

3. **Improvement**: The team leader continuously works with team members to creatively and innovatively identify ways by which improvement can be achieved.

4. **Contact**: The team leader maintains close contact and open communication with employees and key people in other work units.

5. **Relationships**: The team leader ensures that harmonious work relationships are maintained within the team and with others and constructively resolves conflict.

6. **Development**: The team leader places emphasis on developing new skills and competencies both for him or her and for members of the team.

7. **Team Interaction**: The team leader is a team player who shares responsibility and recognition with other members of the team.

8. **Personal Characteristics**: The team leader sets a personal model of conduct and behavior for other team members to follow.

Summary

The most successful managers, supervisors and other work group leaders are those who understand the nature of group dynamics and who use this knowledge to transform the employees in their work groups into a winning team.

Because people have strong social and affiliation needs groups are inevitable. When groups form they usually exhibit characteristics which can be distinguished from the characteristics of the individuals who make up groups. For example, all groups have a <u>common purpose</u>, share <u>common attitudes</u>, have <u>unity</u>, <u>social control</u>, and possess a <u>structure</u>. Groups can be either formal or informal. Formal groups are either appointed or elected while informal groups simply evolve within formal groups. However, both informal groups and informal leaders can exert strong influence over other group members and can significantly affect group performance.

Groups are not necessarily teams. Teams are different from groups in that not only do teams have the group characteristics but in addition team members share a degree of loyalty, commitment, responsibility and openness that enables them to achieve problem solving synergism. These additional qualities are what create and maintain winning teams.

Leaders of winning teams must function more like a coach and facilitator than like a traditional manager or supervisor. In order to do this the most successful winning team leaders have been found to regularly engage in constructive team building behaviors that focus on Action, Performance, Improvement, Contact, Relationships, Development, Team Interaction and Personal Characteristics of the team leader.

Building A Winning Team Self-Awareness Test

Instructions: Decide whether each of the statements below is true **(T)**, false **(F)** or whether you are uncertain **(?)** about it. Indicate your decision by placing a mark in the appropriate column to the right of each statement.

		T	?	F
01.	I take prompt action to correct problems that could affect my team.	☐	☐	☐
02.	My employees see me as a coach and a facilitator.	☐	☐	☐
03.	I maintain close contact with my peers in other work groups.	☐	☐	☐
04.	I frequently meet with my employees as a team to discuss how we can improve our work operations.	☐	☐	☐
05.	I encourage my subordinates to be creative.	☐	☐	☐
06.	My employees freely exchange job related information with employees in other work groups.	☐	☐	☐
07.	We resolve any disagreement or conflict through discussion and problem solving.	☐	☐	☐
08.	My employees receive continuous training in the job skills they need to meet new challenges.	☐	☐	☐
09.	All of the employees in my work group are involved making decisions that affect them and their work.	☐	☐	☐
10.	My personal competence and work ethic help to motivate my employees.	☐	☐	☐

Personal Developmental Plan

Prepare a development plan to improve your team building skills by answering the following questions:

A.   The team building skills that I use most frequently and that are currently my greatest strengths are:

B.   The team building skills in which I currently need the greatest improvement are:

C.   My personal objectives for improving my team building skills are:

D.   The specific strategies by which I plan to develop and strengthen my team building skills are (use additional paper if necessary):

   1.

   2.

   3.

   4.

   5.

Chapter 4
Communicating And Active Listening

> ## Learning Objectives
> **After completing this chapter you will have learned:**
>
> What communication is and how the process of communication works.
>
> How to avoid common barriers to communication.
>
> How to improve two-way communication with others by developing active listening skill.

Communication is most commonly defined as the sharing of information among two or more people. However, in some cases, such as when someone writes a message or records one on an audio cassette or CD, the actual sharing of communication might not take place at the same time that it is initiated.

Key Point
Communication can be defined as the sharing of information among two or more people.

The most common of communication is the spoken word or verbal communication. Communication also commonly takes the form of the written word or symbol. But there are other forms as well like art, music, computer graphics, physical contact, facial expressions and other "body language," or non-verbal forms. Communication exists whenever one or more persons convey a message of any type or in any form to another person.

Some managers and supervisors have a very narrow perspective of communication. They tend to see it as being a predominantly downward process useful for issuing orders. Communication is much broader than that and has many different purposes and objectives. Among its many purposes are to inform, to persuade, to entertain, to understand, to instruct and to stimulate action.

Key Point
Among the purposes of communication are to inform, to persuade, to entertain, to understand, to instruct and to stimulate action.

To inform --This is perhaps the most common purpose or objective of communication. When we inform, we provide facts, opinions, feelings and attitudes and share these with others. Stock market quotations, financial reports, objective reporting on current events, sales reports, statistical quality control data and personnel attendance records are facts. Editorials, letters to the editor, employee opinion survey data, performance appraisals (other than MBO and other objectives oriented forms), and political polls are all examples of opinion, attitude or other perceptual information. Yet, they all have the common purpose of informing people.

To Persuade -- You can (and probably have) used communication for the purpose of "Selling" your ideas. You persuade others to follow your point of view or to take certain action. Politicians make speeches to persuade the public to vote for them. Supervisors and managers sometimes "sell" or persuade employees to adopt procedures or practices. The clergy preach to persuade their congregation in matters of faith and salesmen use communication to persuade customers to buy their products.

To Entertain -- Communication is used to entertain us in many ways; e.g. radio, television, and motion pictures. Training videos and other audio visual aids are often made entertaining to maintain interest and attention and to enhance their communication value.

To Understand -- You can use communication to help others understand your meaning or intent or to inquire so that you can understand others. Sometimes mangers and supervisors place too much emphasis on getting their own point of view across to others and not enough on listening and understanding others. In order to fully understand, you must have well developed listening skills. When you communicate with others, be sure to give equal attention to understanding them as well as to being understood yourself.

To Instruct -- Communication is obviously critical to the entire process of education. At work you will see communication used in this regard most commonly in on-the-job training for employees, apprenticeship programs, technical workshops, meetings to explain and instruct employees about policies, procedures and work rules and in connection with management and supervisory skill development programs.

To Stimulate Action -- In most cases, communication is not complete without stimulating action or eliciting a response. The people with whom you communicate might agree or disagree with you. They might challenge or support you, laugh or express anger, cast a vote, follow an instruction, carry out a work assignment or file a complaint. But, almost invariably, your communication will, and should, result in some kind of response action.

Key Point
In order for communication to take place there must be a message, a sender, a receiver and a communication medium.

In order for communication to take place, there must be a message, a sender, and a receiver. There must also be a medium for communication; a way by which the message is transmitted. For example, messages can be transmitted verbally and non-verbally through audio, visual or digital means. (Other technical means are also possible but are not within the scope of this book.) Employees in most organizations use person-to-person meetings, telephone, email, letters, computers, video, cell phones, flip charts, memos, and similar means to convey messages. Once transmitted, communication is processed through channels like the chain-of-command, through small group department meetings, general assemblies, over intranet systems, and even through the grapevine.

Communication begins with the sender who has a message that he or she wants to send to someone else. The message is a thought that the sender wants to convey to the receiver. The sender must encode or translate the thought into a message form that will be understood by the receiver. This means that the sender must transform his or her thought into sound (words), symbols (letters of the alphabet, pictures, etc.), or some other transmittable message form. Also, any message that the sender transmits will be affected by his or her personality, perceptions, intelligence, language fluency, vocabulary and many similar factors. The message is transmitted through an environment that requires the selection of media and channels for message transmission. The sender must decide how best to "communicate" the message; saying it to the receiver in person or over the telephone, writing an email, passing it along through subordinate-level supervisors at department meetings or communicating it some other way. Finally, the receiver must accurately receive and decipher the message. In doing this, the receiver is acting on the basis of his or her own attitudes, perceptions, beliefs and personality. The communication loop is closed when the receiver provides feedback to the sender.

Communication Model

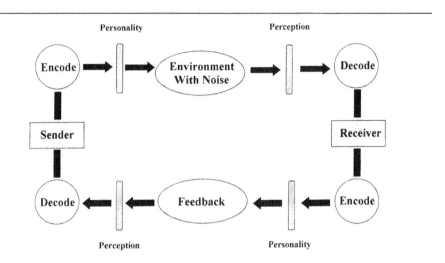

Key Point
Receivers receive messages through the screen of their personality, attitudes, perceptions and beliefs.

Throughout this process there is the potential for many external barriers that could have a negative affect on the transmission and reception of the message. Noise, static, distraction, business conditions, other people, mechanical breakdowns, postal delays, errors and act of God can all combine to hinder the seemingly simple act of conveying a message. When one considers all of these potential barriers and hindrances it is amazing that effective communication is possible at all!

Earlier in this chapter, you learned that various barriers can affect the quality of communication. Certain barriers are within the person of both the sender and receiver; e.g., personality, perception, attitude, etc. Others, such as noise, distraction, and the like are external in origin. Two additional aspects of the communication process, meanings and semantics, are at the foundation of effective communication but, if not carefully considered, can become communication barriers

One of the most difficult tasks that a sender must deal with is clearly encoding a thought into a form that will be understood by the receiver. This is extremely difficult because meaning is only achieved by a joint process between two or more parties to communication.

For example, you might have seen the old cartoon in which two psychiatrists pass each other on the street, each saying "good morning." The next frame of the cartoon shows both psychiatrists saying to themselves, "I wonder what he meant by that?" The point of this anecdote is that often even under the best and most innocent of conditions, communication senders and receivers have considerable difficulty getting together on the same "wavelength." What the sender says or writes might not really be what he or she means. What the receiver hears or reads is often not what the sender meant. Then, to compound the issue even further, there is the problem of semantics. The sender must be very careful to select the proper word or term to describe his or her thought. Care must be taken to ensure that the word or term that is selected is not only accurate, but that it is compatible with the receiver's intellectual, cultural and societal capacity to decode it. Slang, jargon, shop terms or local colloquialisms are potentially dangerous. If you use them be very careful to consider how they will be understood by the receiver.

After exhaustive studies which involved interviewing thousands of workers on the job, researchers at Loyola University concluded that "... of all the sources of information a manager has by which he or she can come to know and accurately size up the personalities of the people in his or her department, listening to the individual employee is the most important. The most stereotyped report that we have received from thousands of workers who testified that they liked their supervisor was the one: "I like my boss, he listens to me, I can talk to him.

Key Point
An effective listening skill is one of the most important human relations skills a leader can acquire.

Effective listening is one of the most important human skills a manager, supervisor or other work group leader can acquire. With the possible exception of a basic, sincere respect for the personal dignity and worth of our fellow human being, accompanied by practicing the "golden rule"; i.e., treat others as you, yourself, want to be treated, listening has the greatest day-to-day impact of any of these skills on relationships with others. It is essentially impossible to interact with another human being without communicating with him or her in one way or another. Effective communication is not possible without effective listening. However, a group of researchers at Ohio State University conducted a study to determine how effectively the average person listens. The results showed that the average person's listening effectiveness was only 25%. Astounded and disbelieving, the researchers repeated the study. The results were the same. The average person really listens to only 25% of what he or she hears.

The major reason for this is the prevalence of listening barriers throughout the communication process. If you have ever wondered why you have trouble understanding others or wondered why they sometimes fail to understand you, then you should learn about barriers to listening effectiveness. Among the more common barriers to listening effectiveness are lack of attention and interest, bias and prejudice, distraction and defensiveness. However, perhaps the most serious barrier is the tendency for people to listen to others judgmentally -- to prejudge the speaker's message. The remedy for this is **Active Listening**.

Key Point
Active listening is the ability to listen and respond to others in a non-evaluative way that encourages further communication.

According to author and management educator Dennis C. Kinlaw active listening has these three elements:

1. "It is the ability to receive accurately the whole message sent by another person; i.e., the entire verbal, non-verbal and emotional content of a message;

2. It is the ability to convey to another person by ones own verbal and nonverbal behavior that one is listening; and

3. It is the ability to encourage another person to continue to speak and build information."

The key concept here is that when we listen to others evaluatively we are not really listening to understand but rather to judge. This leads us to respond to others judgmentally and to act the same way. Now, let's put all of this together. Here are seven easy-to-follow tips that will help you improve communication with your subordinates, peers and superiors!

Choose The Message Carefully -- Be sure that you know exactly what you want to communicate and what you want the message to accomplish. Keep it simple and to the point.

Target The Communication Accurately -- Decide for whom the message is intended. Be sure to get the right message to the right person.

Select Proper Channels And Media -- Determine the best way to send the message. Decide whether it should be verbal or written and whether it should be sent by telephone, FAX, email, cell phone (twitter) in person or some other way.

Anticipate And Avoid Communication Barriers -- Identify potential barriers that could interfere with the successful communication of the message. Avoid or minimize these problems before they can occur.

Send The Message Effectively -- Be clear and concise when transmitting the message. Think of ways that will make it easier for the receiver to understand the message. Use graphics, pictures or other aids to help make the message more understandable.

Get Feedback -- Learn if the message was received and understood in the way that you intended. Get feedback about whether or not it accomplished its purpose.

Learn From Mistakes -- If a problem occurs analyze the situation to find out why. Use this information to avoid the same problem next time.

Summary

Communication is the sharing of information among two or more people. It takes both verbal and non-verbal forms. The key elements of the communication process are a sender, a message and a receiver. The sender encodes or translates a thought into a message, transmits it to a receiver over communication media and through channels. Then, the receiver must accurately decode the message and take some kind of response action. When a sender encodes and transmits a message, he or she must be very careful to select words or terms that accurately convey the desired meaning and must be sensitive both to his or her own and the receiver's predispositions, all of which can affect the accurate decoding of the message.

The skill of effectively listening to his or her employees has been considered to be the most important source of information that a supervisor can acquire. Because of this, listening skill might well be the single most important human relations skill. Unfortunately, the listening effectiveness of the average person is only about 25%.

There are many potential barriers to communication but the most serious is the tendency for people to listen to others evaluatively. When this is done the listener does not listen to understand but rather to judge the speaker's message. Judgmental listening leads to the listener responding and acting in a judgmental manner.

In order to improve communication with others, managers, supervisors and other work group leaders should develop the skill of active listening and engage in positive communication behaviors like choosing their message carefully, accurately targeting the audience, selecting proper communication channels and obtaining feedback.

Communicating And Active Listening Self-Awareness Test

Instructions: Decide whether each of the statements below is true **(T)**, false **(F)** or whether you are uncertain **(?)** about it. Indicate your decision by placing a mark in the appropriate column to the right of each statement.

		T	?	F
01.	All communication involves the processing of written or verbal messages that are exchanged between people.	☐	☐	☐
02.	The purposes of communication are to inform, to persuade, to entertain, to instruct and to stimulate action.	☐	☐	☐
03.	The listening effectiveness of the average person is about 50% to 75%.	☐	☐	☐
04.	Carefully worded letters and memos are the most effective way to communicate with employees.	☐	☐	☐
05.	The main communication responsibility of a leader is to provide job related information to employees.	☐	☐	☐
06.	The grapevine is an excellent way to communicate with employees.	☐	☐	☐
07.	About 60% of communication context is conveyed through non-verbal means like body language.	☐	☐	☐
08.	Active listening requires responding to others in a way that encourages further communication.	☐	☐	☐
09.	Silence can be effective tool for stimulating further communication from the other person.	☐	☐	☐
10.	Listening is the most important supervisory skill.	☐	☐	☐

Personal Developmental Plan

Prepare a development plan to improve your communication skills by answering the following questions:

A. The communication skills that I use most frequently and that are currently my greatest strengths are:

B. The communication skills in which I currently need the greatest improvement are:

C. My personal objectives for improving my communication skills are:

D. The specific strategies by which I plan to develop and strengthen my communication skills are (use additional paper if necessary):

   1.

   2.

   3.

   4.

   5.

Chapter 5
Motivating Through Empowerment

Learning Objectives

After completing this chapter you will have learned:

What empowerment is and how it can affect employee work performance and overall organization effectiveness.

Six key steps that are necessary to create an empowered work force.

What you can do to become a facilitative leader and motivate your employees by empowering them.

Recognizing that they must find a more effective way to improve performance and meet the challenges of foreign competition, many North American organizations have experimented with alternative ways of dealing with their work forces. One approach that has gained in popularity is the process of empowerment. Empowerment is a name for a set of principles developed earlier in this century which are now being used more effectively to enhance the value of employees' contribution to the attainment of organizational goals.

From the 1890s through the early part of the twentieth century most organizations, especially in the manufacturing industry, relied on Frederick Taylor's concept of scientific management to achieve increases in labor productivity. However, primary reliance on scientific management waned after the famous Hawthorne studies at Westinghouse demonstrated the importance of the human factor in organization performance. During the 1940's and 1950's increased attention was given to human relations theory and in 1961 Douglas McGregor published his findings regarding the assumptions that managers make about employees, *Theory X* and *Theory Y.*

According to McGregor's Theory Y assumptions, employees "will exercise self-direction and self-control in the service of objectives to which (they are) committed." Theory Y also suggests that "the average human learns, under proper conditions, not only to accept but to seek responsibility." That same year management scientist Rensis Likert published his Systems Four theory which held that productivity is closely linked to supportive behavior by supervision and to participative management practices.

During the 1960's and 1970's, the United States and other Western societies experienced a dramatic change in the attitudes, perceptions and expectations of the work force. Youth entering the work force had fundamentally different attitudes about such issues as authority, the work ethic, social values, productivity and other aspects that were traditional within large bureaucratic organization; i.e. "Big Business."

The impact of the emerging work force on these traditional forces was so strong that since the 1980s a new wave of corporate social responsibility has been introduced together with increased emphasis on the quality of work life (QWL). From the 1990s to the present time, an increasing number of organizations in the United States and in other countries updated their business philosophies and practices to be in conformance with ISO 9000 and ISO 14000 standards and with the now popular LEAD and Six Sigma principals (discussed more fully in Chapter 12 of this book). The concept of empowerment, that has been shown to increase employee motivation and commitment and to boost lagging quality and productivity, is an important tenant of these programs.

Key Point
In an empowered work force power, responsibility, information and decisions are expanded and shared more widely.

Employee empowerment is set of work relationship interactions in which power, responsibility, information, decisions, and are expanded and shared more widely among management, supervision and employees -- all who are collaborating to achieve a common goal. The underlying concept of empowerment is very similar to the philosophies of McGregor's Theory Y and Likert's System Four cited earlier. Stated in a more contemporary way, employees will be more committed to an organization's goals if they perceive that they have the power to influence their work environment. Their motivation to meet or exceed performance goals will be enhanced by facilitative leadership and by participation in decision making and problem solving.

Key Point
Empowerment requires that managers, supervisors and other leaders change their way of interacting with employees.

By increasing the involvement of employees in problem solving and decision making, by encouraging them to be creative and innovative and by adding flexibility and responsibility to the work place, management can tap an enormous reserve of employee energy, commitment and performance excellence. However, in order to do this certain organization climate conditions must be established. Also, managers, supervisors and other leaders must adopt a role and a set of behaviors which differ considerably from the traditional way of dealing with employees.

Key Point
Empowered employees are more involved in decision making and problem solving and have greater control over their work.

As a manager, supervisor or other organizational leader here is what must be done in order to motivate your employees through empowerment:

Develop an Open Communication System

Communication among employees in an empowered work group is open, honest and candid. It is a two-way process in which the leader ensures that his or her employees have all the information they need to do their jobs properly and in which mutual feedback is provided about work performance, job related problems and accomplishments.

Focus on Total Quality and Continuous Improvement

Empowered employees share a determination to produce the highest possible quality product or service; one that fully meets the needs and expectations of their internal and external customers. They also are continuously looking for ways to improve the quality and effectiveness of their work performance. Leaders of empowered employees actively solicit their ideas for change and improvement.

Enhance the Nature of Employees' Jobs

Empowerment exists when employees have meaningful work and when they have a sense of competency. Continuous job skill training, performance coaching, job enrichment and other techniques can also be used by leaders to increase the positive attitude of employees toward their jobs. In addition, within reasonable parameters, empowered employees are given increased responsibility, power and control over the way their jobs are performed.

Develop Work Teams

Teamwork is the essence of empowerment. Empowered employees work as a team to make decisions and to solve problems. They cooperate and collaborate to achieve a common goal. As a team, empowered employees share responsibility for the performance of the work group's task or mission. They share recognition and rewards for accomplishing work unit objectives.

Practice Facilitative Leadership

Empowered work teams respond best to facilitative leadership in which the leader is a coach and a trainer rather than a judge and an evaluator. Facilitative leaders are concerned equally about people and performance. They guide, support and encourage employees rather than tell them what to do and direct them in how they should do it. Facilitative leaders are also effective team leaders.

Maintain Supportive Work Conditions

In order to be effective, employees in empowered work groups must have the tools, equipment, supplies and physical work conditions they need to do their jobs properly. Facilitative leaders are also good planners who effectively organize the various resources that their work teams need to accomplish their objectives.

Employee empowerment can be an effective way for organizations to increase productivity and profitability. However, in order to be successful empowerment requires a major cultural change within organizations; a completely different way of thinking about employees and of interacting with them. This may not be suitable for all organizations. In fact, there is considerable recent evidence suggesting that without the necessary cultural change efforts to implement organization-wide empowerment programs can fail badly. Empowerment can be a powerful and constructive tool for positive change. But it is not a panacea that will cure bad management practices.

Key Point
Any manager, supervisor or other organizational leader can use empowerment techniques successfully.

Does this mean that without an organization-wide cultural change you personally cannot use empowerment to improve the effectiveness of your own work group? Not at all!

Empowerment techniques can be practiced by any manager, supervisor or work group leader quite successfully. Moreover, the chances are that once other leaders see the results you and your work group are achieving through empowerment they will want to try it, also.

Summary

Employee empowerment is a way of thinking about employees and of interacting with them that is based on proven leadership practices that were developed by leading management scientists earlier in this century and that has been refined through the years to the present time. Empowerment theory recognizes that the creative, innovative and productive capacity of employees can be tapped more effectively if they are more involved in making decisions and exercising control over work activities that directly affect them.

A key principle of empowerment is the concept of shared responsibility in which power, responsibility for task performance, information and decisions are shared more widely among work group members who together collaborate to accomplish a common goal. Although empowerment practices can be used effectively by any manager, supervisor or other organizational leader, in order for empowerment to be most successful the proper organizational conditions must be set, including an organization-wide cultural change. Conditions that support empowerment include:

- developing an open communication system
- focusing on total quality and continuous improvement
- enhancing the nature of employees' jobs
- developing work teams
- practicing facilitative leadership
- maintaining supportive physical work conditions

When all of these conditions exist, the process of empowerment can be used to significantly increase the value of employees' contributions to achieving organizational goals.

Motivating Through Empowerment Self-Awareness Test

Instructions: Decide whether each of the statements below is true **(T)**, false **(F)** or whether you are uncertain **(?)** about it. Indicate your decision by placing a mark in the appropriate column to the right of each statement.

		T	?	F
01.	All of my employees have the information that they need to do their jobs properly.	☐	☐	☐
02.	I regularly obtain feedback from my employees about their job-related problems.	☐	☐	☐
03.	My employees understand how their performance affects the quality of our products or services.	☐	☐	☐
04.	The average employee in my work group is willing to seek out responsibility.	☐	☐	☐
05.	My employees share responsibility for producing a high quality product.	☐	☐	☐
06.	I am considered to be a good coach and trainer.	☐	☐	☐
07.	I continuously train my employees to improve their performance and increase their job skills.	☐	☐	☐
08.	I encourage my employees to be creative.	☐	☐	☐
09.	The focus in our work group is on getting the job done through teamwork and collaboration.	☐	☐	☐
10.	All of the employees in my work group are involved in making decisions that affect them.	☐	☐	☐

Personal Developmental Plan

Prepare a development plan to improve your empowerment skills by answering the following questions:

A. The empowerment skills that I use most frequently and that are currently my greatest strengths are:

B. The empowerment skills in which I currently need the greatest improvement are:

C. My personal objectives for improving my empowerment skills are:

D. The specific strategies by which I plan to develop and strengthen my empowerment skills are (use additional paper if necessary):

    1.

    2.

    3.

    4.

    5.

Chapter 6
Solving Problems Effectively

Learning Objectives

After completing this chapter you will have learned:

The relationship between problem solving and decision making.

How to use a basic six-step model to solve problems and make decisions.

What the common causes of conflict are and how to resolve conflict constructively.

One of the most important responsibilities of both individual employees and of work groups as teams is to solve problems. Individual employees continuously are required to solve technical, administrative, sales, and customer service problems that arise within their areas of responsibility. Work groups and task teams must solve production, quality, productivity, morale and other problems. Managers, supervisors and other work group leaders must not only facilitate effective problem within their work groups but in addition must occasionally resolve interpersonal conflict and employee performance problems.

Key Point
Problem solving is a basic and important responsibility of both individual employees and of work groups as teams.

All problem solving requires that a decision be made. The process by which problems are solved and by which decisions are made is very similar. Because of this good problem solvers are also usually good decision makers. Unfortunately, less than 50% of all managers, supervisors and other work group leaders are good problem solvers. The reason for this is that less than 50% of these leaders use a systematic method when solving a problem.

Key Point
Ineffective problem solving is usually caused by the failure to use a systematic problem solving method.

Many proprietary problem solving systems have been developed to help leaders and employees improve their problem solving skills. Some are very easy to use while others are more complicated. However, almost all of them follow these basic systematic steps:

1. Define the Problem

Failure to accurately define or determine the real problem or decision issue is a major reason why many problem solving efforts are ineffective. In order to overcome this barrier it is necessary to distinguish between a symptom and the true nature of the problem. In most cases this can be done by first writing a general description of the overall problem situation. Then, break the "fuzzy" problem situation into its components and look for the component that seems to be the primary cause of all of the other components.

Key Point
The crucial first step in most systematic problem solving methods is to define the problem or decision issue.

2. Gather the Facts

Before a problem can be rationally tackled the facts about it must be known. In some cases, especially with technical problems like those related to quality improvement, it is possible to gather problem related facts by using data collection aids like charts and graphs (process flow charts, histograms, control charts, etc.). In other cases, information can be collected through personal observation, employee records, personal interviews and by asking diagnostic questions like how, what, when, where, why, how much, how fast, and so on. The accuracy of your problem solving efforts depends to a large extent on how much accurate information you have about the problem.

3. **Analyze the Problem**

Problems are usually variances from desired outcomes. In order to understand the variance it is first necessary to clearly understand what should happen and also what is happening. The difference between what should happen and what is happening is the variance or the problem.

Key Point
Most problems can be identified by determining the variance between what is happening and what should be happening.

The next step is to determine why the variance occurred. This means looking for the problem root cause -- not for its symptoms. There are several useful techniques like cause-effect diagraming that help identify problem root causes, but a very simple aid is the "why" technique.

This method begins with the clearly defined variance or precisely stated problem. The sequence of "why" technique questions can best be illustrated by an example in which the problem or variance was found to be:

> "Response time to customer inquiries about the status of their orders now averages 3 hours. The best employees respond with 30 minutes and the standard for response time is 1 hour."

Why is the average response time 3 hours?

a. "Because there are many new, inexperienced employees in the customer service section."

Why are there many new, inexperienced employees ...."

> (1) "Because many of the more experience employees have left the company."
>
> **Why have many of the more experienced ...."**
>
> (a) Because they felt that they had little control over their job and that no one was interested in their opinions."
> **Why did they feel ....**

Obviously, the example is leading in a direction that would probably indicate weak leadership in the customer service section, failure to listen to employees' problems and concerns, an absence of empowerment, etc. Note that there may be more than one answer to the initial "why" question and that response would have to be followed using the "why" technique, also.

4. Develop Alternative Solutions

Once the root cause of the problem has been identified alternative solutions must be developed. One effective and easy-to-use method to do this is through brainstorming. Brainstorming is a technique in which the objective is to develop as many alternative solutions as possible in a short period of time.

Key Point
Brainstorming is an effective and easy-to-use method to develop alternative solutions to a problem.

The key is to make a written list of ideas without pausing to evaluate, make judgments, or to ask questions for purpose of clarification. Wild, creative ideas and quantity are desired. Evaluation and the elimination of duplicates take place **after** the brainstorming session has ended. The most promising alternatives are then studied further.

5. Evaluate the Alternatives

When evaluating solutions, many factors such as cost, labor, resources available, effort involved, affect on morale and other short term and long range effects must be considered. For example, if a solution is extremely expensive to the organization it may not be practical. But if the basic idea can be kept and a less costly method discovered then the solution may become more feasible.

One easy-to-use method for evaluating alternative solutions is to develop a set of evaluation criteria, judgment standards, and then rate each alternative against each criterion. A simple rating 1 to 5 rating scale can be used for this purpose; e.g. 1 = Poor while 5 = Excellent. Alternative solutions are then ranked according to the sum of their scores.

6. Decide and Act

It should be remembered that whichever method is used to help evaluate alternative solutions there is no substitute for judgment. In many cases two or more alternatives may be ranked so closely that the numerical difference is not significant. Ultimately, the work group leader or the problem solving team must decide which is the best solution and they must act to implement it. Solution implementation requires planning, organizing, communicating, coordinating, follow-up and control -- all components of the management cycle. It also involves anticipating barriers to solution implementation (like apathy, resistance to change, hidden personal agenda and fear) and preparing ways by which those barriers can be overcome.

The follow-up of a solution can take many forms, depending upon all the factors relating to it. It may be a short written report evaluating the solution and its effects. Or, with a very complex decision, the evaluation may be lengthy and detailed. In any event, information must be obtained to measure the effects of the solution.

Problem solving can be accomplished by individual employees within an organization acting alone or it can be done by employees collaboratively in a team environment. The same basic six-step process is followed in either case. However, when employees engage in team problem solving they must also use effective team interaction skills. This means that they must be sure to include and involve all of the team's resources in the problem solving effort. They must use active listening skills, encourage the full participation of all team members and apply the empowerment principle of shared responsibility. Team problem solving is usually more time consuming than solving a problem as an individual contributor. However, team problem solving can be far more effective and the team process enhances commitment to the problem solution.

Key Point
Team problem solving may be more time consuming than problem solving by individuals; but it is usually more effective.

Problem solving is often thought of as applying to "thing" or systems problems such as technical systems, financial matters, administrative procedures, work processes and other organizational systems. However, the same basic problem solving model shown above can also apply to human problems like interpersonal conflict and employee work performance deficiencies. The problem solving process is basically the same; only the details are different. For example, when non-productive conflict occurs among individuals it is still necessary to first accurately define the nature of the problem or the specific dispute issue. Facts about the disagreement must be gathered and studied. The root cause or causes of the conflict must be identified and alternative solutions developed. These solutions must then be evaluated to determine which is best and the best solution must be selected and implemented. One difference is that unlike many other types of problems, the fundamental causes of conflict are known, as are alternative approaches to conflict resolution. In most cases interpersonal conflict is caused by:

Communication Misunderstandings -- The message sender communicating only within the framework of his or her own background, values system, culture and perception set and/or the message being received through similar screens and barriers.

Role Perceptions -- Two or more people having different perceptions about the nature and scope of their respective organizational roles and responsibilities, which are in conflict with the other's perceptions.

Conflicting Goals -- Non-congruent goals and objectives, usually personal, in which the actions of one person is perceived to be a threat to goal attainment by the other person.

Bias and Prejudice -- Gender, age, ethnic, racial, religious or other social prejudice.

Personality Differences -- Personal likes and dislikes regarding one's personality characteristics and traits, ethical standards, behavioral characteristics and personal mannerisms.

There are four major approaches to dealing with conflict: avoidance, power, compromise and problem solving. Many people use avoidance. They simply try to avoid contact with those that they are in conflict. In the work place it may not be possible to avoid the other person, especially if the antagonists are interdependent members of the same work group. Besides, avoidance avoids the problem, it does not solve it.

Power is sometimes used by rivals to overcome the other person or to suppress the conflict, especially when used by a superior against a subordinate. Like avoidance, power does not solve problems. In fact, in most cases power increases the severity of the conflict because it establishes winners and losers. Compromise may seem like a stem in the right direction. However, in order for compromise to take place both parties to a conflict must give up something they believe is theirs. Moreover, the basic, underlying cause of the conflict is still not resolved.

Key Point
Problem solving is the only truly effective way to resolve conflict. All other strategies fail to resolve the underlying conflict cause.

Problem solving is the only truly effective method for resolving conflict. Problem solving identifies the root cause of the conflict and develops a workable solution that will resolve it. The solution must be workable because when two or more people participate in problem solving activities they must reach consensus as to the best solution. Consensus means that they both agree that it is the best and that they will commit themselves to the solution. Lastly, problem solving also applies to employee performance problems. This subject, however, will be discussed elsewhere in this program.

Summary

Individual employees, members of work teams, managers, supervisors and other work group leaders are continually required to solve problems and make decisions. Problems cannot be solved without also making decisions. The process for solving problems and for making decisions is essentially the same. Even though problem solving is a crucial skill for leaders less than 50% of all managers, supervisors and other work group leaders are effective problem solvers. This is because less than 50% use a systematic method when solving a problem or making a decision.

While problem solving methods may vary, they all share the following six elements:

1. Define the Problem
2. Gather the Facts
3. Analyze the Problem
4. Develop Alternative Solutions
5. Evaluate the Alternatives
6. Decide and Act

Problem solving is accomplished not only by individual contributors but also by employees in groups and teams. Team problem solving usually takes longer than problem solving by individuals but it can be much more effective. The problem solving model discussed in this chapter can be used not only for "thing" and systems problems but also for human problems like resolving interpersonal conflict or correcting employee performance deficiencies. The process for solving these types of problems is the same, although each application is different is certain respects.

The basic causes of conflict are known to fall into one or more categories such as communication misunderstandings, role perceptions, conflicting goals, bias and prejudice and personality differences. Similarly, there are four common approaches to conflict resolution including avoidance, power, compromise and problem solving. Only problem solving among these approaches can truly resolve conflict.

The six-step problem solving model in this chapter also applies to employee performance problems which are discussed more fully elsewhere in this book.

Solving Problems Effectively Self-Awareness Test

Instructions: Decide whether each of the statements below is true **(T)**, false **(F)** or whether you are uncertain **(?)** about it. Indicate your decision by placing a mark in the appropriate column to the right of each statement.

		T	?	F
01.	Solving problems and making decisions require the same basic skills.	☐	☐	☐
02.	Problem solving always involves making a decision and decision making always involves solving a problem.	☐	☐	☐
03.	The majority of all managers and supervisors are skilled problem solvers and decision makers.	☐	☐	☐
04.	A problem is the variance between what is and what should be.	☐	☐	☐
05.	The first step in most problem solving methods is to carefully analyze the problem.	☐	☐	☐
06.	The criteria for evaluating which solution is best may vary from problem to problem.	☐	☐	☐
07.	The basic problem solving method used by teams is considerably different from that used by individuals.	☐	☐	☐
08.	Compromise is a good conflict resolution strategy.	☐	☐	☐
09.	Conflict resolution strategies and methods differ from systematic problem solving methods.	☐	☐	☐
10.	Systematic problem solving methods are not suitable for employee performance problems.	☐	☐	☐

Personal Developmental Plan

Prepare a development plan to improve your problem solving skills by answering the following questions:

A. The problem solving skills that I use most frequently and that are currently my greatest strengths are:

B. The problem solving skills in which I currently need the greatest improvement are:

C. My personal objectives for improving my problem solving skills are:

D. The specific strategies by which I plan to develop and strengthen my problem solving skills are (use additional paper if necessary):

   1.

   2.

   3.

   4.

   5.

Chapter 7
Improving Planning Skills

Learning Objectives

After completing this chapter you will have learned:

The purpose and importance of planning and organizing.

How to set meaningful and valid objectives.

Key principles of time management

Most organizations have a formal planning process. Long range strategic plans, organization policies, procedures, methods, schedules, work rules and budgets are all components or products of an organization's planning process. Planning is the first of the four basic management functions. The others are organizing, directing and controlling. Planning is an activity that requires the use of conceptual skills. Planning is extremely important because it is a skill that serves as a major determinant of managerial effectiveness. People who lack planning skills tend to find themselves constantly "putting out fires" or resorting to crisis management tactics.

Key Point
Planning is a very important skill because it serves as a major determinant of managerial effectiveness.

Planning involves setting objectives and then developing strategies or a plan by which the objectives can be accomplished. It is a prerequisite to the other components of the Management Cycle. Planning also applies to one's own activities, such as setting priorities and scheduling work, or to the activities of many others within the organization.

The first step in the planning process is to anticipate or forecast future events. For example, the senior management of an organization might envision corporate growth, the need for a total quality management program or the desirability of moving the organization in the direction of self-directed work teams. Once a vision (or organizational mission) is clarified it is necessary to set specific objectives or goals which represent the results needed in order to transform the vision into a tangible outcome.

In order to be valid, objectives must be precise, measurable and realistic. An objective must be a clear statement of what is to be accomplished together with quantitative and qualitative measures that will clearly define when objective accomplishment occurs.

Key Point
In order for an objective to be valid it must be precise, measurable and realistic.

In most cases this means that an objective must include the elements of time, quantity, quality and similar measures. For example, "to improve safety" is much too vague to be a valid objective. What attributes of safety should be improved? "On-the-job" or "off-the-job" accidents? Minor or major injuries? Also, as worded in the example there is no way to measure progress toward accomplishing the objective. Nor is there a way to know whether or not it is realistic.

Let us try again with this objective: "Beginning July 1, 2011, we will establish a program that will reduce the on-the-job, lost time accident rate from 15 to not more than 8 by December 31, 2011." This objective is precise, measurable and probably very realistic or attainable.

Once objectives are set it is necessary to develop a set of strategies, a plan of action, by which they can be accomplished. In most cases, this involves simply listing sequential steps or activities that can be taken to produce the desired results. Referring to the above objective, for example, the following steps might be considered:

1. Conduct a safety audit to identify major types of lost time accidents and their causes.

2. Conduct a safety attitude survey to determine the extent of safety consciousness and awareness among employees.

3. Meet with representatives of the National Safety Council and with the company's worker compensation insurance carrier to obtain their input.

4. Develop an in-house safety training program.

Each of these steps, of course, should be accompanied by beginning and ending dates. Some additional considerations include when the steps or strategies are to be done, who is to do them and what resources are needed. Many of these details are covered in the organizing component of the Management Cycle.

Key Point
Organizing is the gathering of material, monetary, human and other resources needed to make the plan work.

Organizing is the gathering together of the material, monetary, human and other resources needed to make the plan work. When organizing is added to planning, the total process constitutes your entire plan and answers these questions:

- What must be done?
- Why must it be done?
- Where should it be done?
- When should it be done?
- Who should do it?
- How should it be done?

Some supervisors understand how to plan and organize but still have difficulty managing their time and the time of their subordinates. One of the reasons is that they have never learned how to establish priorities and effectively schedule work. In addition, many supervisors fall into a pattern of wasteful time management practices that further inhibit their effectiveness.

Key Point
Time cannot be saved. It can only be used. The key is to use time as effectively as possible.

Time cannot be stretched. There are only 60 minutes in an hour, 24 hours in a day and so on. We can neither make more time nor can we shrink it. Time cannot be saved -- only used. Further, we all have the same amount of time, which is all the time there is. The key is to use time as effectively as possible. Effectively -- not efficiently. It is possible to do unnecessary, time-wasting things very efficiently but the result is ineffectiveness. Remember, work tends to expand to fill whatever time is available.

Any manager, supervisor or other work group leader can easily put together a long list of possible time wasters. Involving the wrong people in meetings, failure to properly prepare before going into a meeting, failure to do it right the first time, and failure to listen non-judgmentally are just a few examples of common time wasters that most people have experienced. More productively, the focus should be on how to make the most effective use of time and in this sense there are two very important tools, prioritization and delegation.

Key Point
One way to ensure that you are investing the proper amount of time is to prioritize your daily work schedule.

One way to ensure that you are investing the proper amount of time to the proper work-related activity is to prioritize your daily work schedule. The best way to do this is, at the beginning of each day, to make a list of all the work activities that you must do. Then, use an "ABC" system to rank the activities. For example, place an "A" next to those items that are "must do's." They have the highest priority because they are essential. Next, place a "B" next to the "should do" items. You can get by if you do not do "B" items but you really should do them. Finally, place a "C" next to the items that would be "nice to do" if time permits. It is OK if you can't get to these items because they can easily be done later.

Once you have assigned priorities to your daily activities make a time log. Break the day into 15 minute intervals. First, schedule all of the "A" items. Make sure that you record them in proper sequence. Then schedule the "B" items, again, in proper sequence. Finally, if you have any remaining time in your schedule list the more important "C" items. If not, or if you can only schedule a few, forget the balance of the "C" items entirely. They're really not that critical anyway.

The second technique that will help you to more effectively manage your own time and that of your employees is delegation. Delegation occurs when you turn a project, or task, totally over to an employee. This means that you give the employee both the responsibility for doing the task and the necessary authority, as well. It makes subordinates responsible for results rather than activities.

Key Point
Delegation makes subordinates responsible for accomplishing results rather than activities.

Do not mistake delegation for making a work assignment. They seem to be similar but they are not necessarily the same. For example, it is a routine work assignment when you ask an employee to perform a particular task, tell him or her how, when, how much and where to do it, closely supervise to make sure that it is being done and retain for yourself the authority to make any relevant decisions. Delegation exists when you ask an employee to do a certain task and then, within proscribed limits, let him or her do what is necessary in order to get the task done - including having the authority to make the necessary decisions.

Knowing when to delegate is just as important as knowing how to delegate. It is a general rule that the task should be done at the lowest level possible. Therefore, whenever a job, project or task arises, ask yourself critically whether you really need to do it personally. Is your personal training, experience, or judgment really needed? Can someone less experienced do the job? If so, then delegate. One last point, delegating does not mean "passing the buck" to a lower level employee. Ultimately, you are the person accountable for the successful operation of your department or section. You, in turn, can and should hold subordinates accountable for the tasks which you have delegated to them. But, don't forget that it is you, not a subordinate, who is answerable to your superior for the overall performance of your work group.

Summary

Planning is the first of four major management functions. It is a prerequisite for all of the other functions because it involves setting the basic objectives of what must be accomplished The first step in the planning process is to anticipate or envision a future event. Objectives are then set in order to transform the vision into a tangible outcome that can be attained. Objectives must be precise, measurable and realistic. The setting of objectives is then followed by developing a plan or a set of strategies by which the objectives can be realized. This step, in turn, is followed by the process of organizing which is gathering together the resources necessary to accomplish the plan.

The planning function is important, but it does not guarantee effectiveness. Even with a workable knowledge of planning, some managers, supervisors and other work group leaders still have difficulty managing their activities because they waste time by not properly preparing for meetings, failing to prioritize work and doing work that could be delegated to subordinates. Many people do not understand that time cannot be saved -- it can only be used. The key is to use time as effectively as possible. One way to make more effective use of time is to set priorities by using an "ABC" system. In this system, the supervisor lists all of his or her daily activities, determines their respective priority and then schedules the activities on the basis of the "must do's" first, "should do's" next, and "nice to do's" last.

The practice of delegation is another essential time management principle. Delegation is the practice of giving subordinates both the responsibility and authority necessary to perform a task; making them responsible for results rather than activities. Delegation does not relieve the supervisor of final accountability for work team performance. Properly used, however, it places task performance at the lowest competent level, thus freeing the supervisor for other duties.

Improving Planning Skills Self-Awareness Test

Instructions: Decide whether each of the statements below is true **(T)**, false **(F)** or whether you are uncertain **(?)** about it. Indicate your decision by placing a mark in the appropriate column to the right of each statement.

		T	?	F
01.	The function of planning requires a greater use of human and technical skills than of conceptual skills.	☐	☐	☐
02.	The first step in the planning process is to set a specific objective.	☐	☐	☐
03.	In order to be valid an objective must be precise, measurable and realistic.	☐	☐	☐
04.	Preparing work schedules for employees and for yourself is a planning activity.	☐	☐	☐
05.	Organizing involves developing plans and gathering the resources that are necessary to implement the plans.	☐	☐	☐
06.	Time management problems can usually be solved by working more effectively, not necessarily more efficiently.	☐	☐	☐
07.	The "ABC" system of prioritization involves listing work activities in alphabetical order.	☐	☐	☐
08.	Delegation involves placing ultimate responsibility for task performance on a subordinate.	☐	☐	☐
09.	There is no way to save time; it can only be used.	☐	☐	☐
10.	A time log is a record of activities broken down by increments of time.	☐	☐	☐

Personal Developmental Plan

Prepare a development plan to improve your planning skills by answering the following questions:

A. The planning skills that I use most frequently and that are currently my greatest strengths are:

B. The planning skills in which I currently need the greatest improvement are:

C. My personal objectives for improving my planning skills are:

D. The specific strategies by which I plan to develop and strengthen my planning skills are (use additional paper if necessary):

   1.

   2.

   3.

   4.

   5.

Chapter 8
Training Employees To Succeed

Learning Objectives

After completing this chapter you will have learned:

The training role of managers, supervisors and other work group leaders.

How to effectively train employees in job skills and make successful work assignments.

How to avoid common training and work assignment pitfalls.

Making training and work assignments is a fundamental responsibility of managers, supervisors and most other work group leaders. But, no matter how willing or motivated an employee might be to meet his or her supervisor's performance expectations, successful task performance is unlikely unless the employee has received proper job training.

Key Point
Making training and work assignments is a key responsibility of managers, supervisors and other work group leaders.

The training responsibility has become even more important during recent years because of today's focus on total quality management. It is further reinforced by the efforts of many organizations to create an empowered work force; training employees to increase their competencies is essential to the concept of employee empowerment. Other reasons why training employees is important include:

- new, inexperienced employees joining the company,
- transferred employees from other departments or classifications,
- improved or revised methods and procedures,
- preparing employees for new technology,
- skill refreshers for more seasoned employees,
- preparing employees for advancement,
- enriching employees' jobs through job rotation,
- developing backups or replacements,
- new equipment and processes,
- revised standards job standards,

and many others reasons.

The importance of your training responsibility can be further understood if you consider that each year billions of dollars are lost in business, industry and public organizations as a direct result of insufficient or improper training of employees. A very high percentage of waste, scrap, rework, low productivity, poor quality, accidents, low morale and, ultimately, lower organizational performance and profitability is directly linked to lack of job knowledge, skill and proficiency caused by training deficiencies.

Key Point
In order to be effective as a trainer, supervisors must have good verbal and non-verbal communication skills.

There is a very close relationship between training and communication. In your role as a trainer your verbal and non-verbal communication skills must be sharp and accurate. It is especially important to form and transmit your training message in a clear, concise and precise way. You must also often use a larger than normal range of non-verbal communication skills. Charts, diagrams, sketches, and other graphics, computer printouts, slides, transparencies and films, demonstrations, and audio or video cassettes are part of the non-verbal communication aids that you may be required to use. Here are some helpful tips that will aid you in improving your overall training effectiveness:

Know your Subject

This means know your job and the job of the person whom you are training. It is not necessary that you be able to do the job of each employee in your work unit better than the incumbent. But, you must know the employee's job well enough to instruct him or her in how it can be performed most effectively.

Understand the Phases of Learning

There are four phases of learning that most people experience. Understanding these phases will help you to become a better trainer.

1. *Unconscious Incompetence*: The learner is not really aware of how much he or she does not know. Teenage boys who boast about how easy it is to drive a car or workers who over confidently take a look at a job and say that it will be "a piece of cake" to do are examples. Your first job here is to make sure that they fully realize how much they have to learn.

2. *Conscious Incompetence*: The employee is in an early learning phase but now recognizes that he or she is not proficient in the task. Employees are more receptive to training at this point.

3. *Conscious Competence*: The employee has now developed skill in the task, but with heavy concentration and effort. He or she can now perform most of the job duties satisfactorily but may require fairly close supervision.

4. *Unconscious Competence*: The employee has learned the job and can perform it proficiently. Close supervision is no longer required.

Communicate Effectively

Use terms and words that will be understood by the employee. Show and demonstrate rather than tell and lecture. Use audio visual aids and get feedback to ensure that the employee really understands what you have taught.

Be Patient

Eventually the person you are training might be able to perform the job far better than you can. But right now his or her knowledge and skills are being developed. Do not push too hard or too fast!

Focus on Practical Application

Perhaps the greatest amount of learning is accomplished through "doing." For example, you can read a book about golf, see films about the subject, and watch golf tournaments. But, if you want to actually play golf you must get out on the golf course driving range and practice. Similarly, in order for your subordinates to really learn how to perform a task they must practice, actually do it.

Follow-Up

Follow up is essential in order to ensure that the trainee has truly learned what you taught and is properly applying learned principles. Personal observation and follow up meetings with the employee is one of the best ways to achieve this.

Key Point
The skill of training subordinates and the skill of making clear work assignments are closely related in several ways.

The skill of training subordinates and the skill of making clear, unambiguous work assignments that employees can and will successfully complete are closely related in several ways. Many supervisors have been frustrated after giving an employee a work assignment that they thought was crystal clear only to have it end in utter confusion or in non-performance.

Some of the potential barriers to making more effective work assignments experienced by supervisors are exactly the same as those that they experience when training employees. These include failure to listen, unwarranted assumptions, failure to ensure that the message (training principle or instruction) was understood, fear of failure, improper message encoding, perceptual differences and impatience on the part of the trainer or supervisor. The issue is that the opportunities for work or training assignments to result in failure are high unless the message sender exercises proper care when he or she encodes and transmits the message.

Even though the process of making work assignments or giving orders has a lot of potential pitfalls, there are ways by which you can increase your chances for success. Here are six steps that will help you to avoid training pitfalls and make more effective work and training assignments:

Plan

Before you approach the employee to give him or her a work assignment make sure that you know what specific result you want accomplished, when the assignment should be done, how, where, with or by whom, what barriers or problems the employee might encounter and, if possible, how these can be overcome. Also consider any other resources, including tools and equipment that will be necessary to properly carry out the work assignment.

Make the Assignment

When you state the work assignment be sure to make it within the framework of the employee's background and experience. Be sensitive to cultural differences and the possibility of inter-cultural misunderstanding. Carefully chose your wording to avoid language or semantics problems and be concise.

Key Point
Bias, prejudice and favoritism are unacceptable practices whenever making training or work assignments.

Be Fair, Uniform and Consistent

Ensure that the assignment is fair, uniform and consistent with the kind of work assignments that you make to other employees who are at the same level and in similar job classifications. Again, bias, prejudice and favoritism are unacceptable practices.

Be Decisive

There is no need to issue a work or training assignment like a dictator. At the same time avoid making the assignment sound as though the employee has the option of refusing it. You can be polite and decisive at the same time.

Verify the Employee's Understanding

Silence does not necessarily indicate understanding; nor, does a "yes" response when a supervisor asks whether an employee understands the assignment. The only sure way to establish that an employee clearly understands an order or instruction is to ask him or her to repeat the assignment back to you.

Facilitate

The key role for today's supervisor is to serve as a coach and a facilitator to help employees in their work groups successfully perform their assigned tasks. Facilitate means to make easier. Also, follow up is not just for control purposes but it is equally to facilitate getting the job done in a way that meets performance standards.

Key Point
Today's supervisor must be a coach and facilitator who helps employees successfully perform their assigned tasks.

At the same time you should remember that you must assume responsibility for the extent to which the employee's assignment has been satisfactorily carried out. You can and should hold the employee responsible for any non-performance on his or her part. But, if the job is not done well your boss will be holding you accountable -- not your subordinate. You can increase chances for successful performance of the work assignment through appropriate supervision and follow-up. How closely you should supervise and how frequently you follow-up will depend on factors such as the complexity of the job, the skill and experience of the employee, and the amount of input required from you.

Summary

The skills of making effective training and work assignments have a lot in common. They both are fundamental responsibilities of any manager, supervisor or other work group leader and they both are very important management and supervisory practices. Both also require effective listening and communication skills.

Training employees in job skills has taken on even greater importance in today's highly competitive economy because of the need to ensure the highest possible levels of product and service quality and labor productivity. Continuous improvement, including on-going employee education and skill development are basic tenants of the current focus on total quality management.

When training employees in new or updated job skills managers, supervisors and other work group leaders increase their effectiveness by knowing the subject well themselves, understanding the phases of learning, communicating clearly, being patient, focusing on the practical application of learned principles and follow up.

There are many reasons why the training and work assignments of some leaders are not carried out properly or not at all. Among the more common reasons are unwarranted assumptions by the supervisor that the employee has understood the assignment, improper message encoding and the absence of verification and feedback. These problems can be overcome by following a six-step method that involves planning, making decisive, fair, uniform and consistent assignments, obtaining feedback to ensure that the assignment was understood and then following up as a coach and facilitator.

Training Employees To Succeed Self-Awareness Test

Instructions: Decide whether each of the statements below is true **(T)**, false **(F)** or whether you are uncertain **(?)** about it. Indicate your decision by placing a mark in the appropriate column to the right of each statement.

		T	?	F
01.	An organization's human resource department should have the major responsibility for training employees.	☐	☐	☐
02.	Training involves considerable use of non-verbal communication skills.	☐	☐	☐
03.	An unconscious incompetent learner is one who passes out during training.	☐	☐	☐
04.	Lecture is a highly effective training method.	☐	☐	☐
05.	Inter-cultural differences among employees have little affect on an organization's training programs.	☐	☐	☐
06.	Failure to properly perform a work assignment is almost always the fault of the employee.	☐	☐	☐
07.	The key role of today's supervisor is to serve as a coach and facilitator who helps employees succeed.	☐	☐	☐
08.	A nod of the head or silence usually indicates that an employee understands the work assignment.	☐	☐	☐
09.	Training assignments should be made on the basis of one's own work background and experience.	☐	☐	☐
10.	There is a close relationship between employee empowerment and developing employees' skills.	☐	☐	☐

Personal Developmental Plan

Prepare a development plan to improve your training skills by answering the following questions:

A. The training skills that I use most frequently and that are currently my greatest strengths are:

B. The training skills in which I currently need the greatest improvement are:

C. My personal objectives for improving my training skills are:

D. The specific strategies by which I plan to develop and strengthen my training skills are (use additional paper if necessary):

   1.

   2.

   3.

   4.

   5.

Chapter 9
Improving Employee Work Performance

Learning Objectives

After completing this chapter you will have learned:

The principles of establishing work standards for employees.

Methods by which you can diagnose employee performance deficiencies.

How to handle persistent employee performance problems.

Ultimately, whether or not an employee performs up to his or her full capability is determined by the employee. Management scientists state that performance is an individual phenomenon. By this they mean that although there are many factors which can influence the quality of an employee's performance, it is the personal motivation, skill, ability and related characteristics of an employee which will really determine his or her performance level. It is the job of each manager, supervisor or other work group leader to understand what factors contribute toward performance and to learn what they can do to improve their employees' performance.

Key Point
Ultimately whether or not an employee performs up to his or her capability is determined by the employee.

Performance is determined by the motivation and ability of the individual employee. Motivation is the willingness of the employee to do the task requested at the desired performance level. Ability is the capability of an employee to perform a task or set of tasks. Ability consists of three major components:

Physical: height, weight, strength, age, audio and visual acuity.

Intellectual: the capability to deal with numbers, verbal skills, conceptual skills, and intelligence.

Psychological: personality, temperament, interests, and attitudes.

Employees will perform at desired levels only if they have the willingness, motivation and ability to do so.

Key Point
Employees will perform at desired performance levels only if they have the willingness, motivation and ability to do so.

There are many factors that can affect the motivation and ability of an employee to perform his or her job. Among these are job design, training, the quality of supervision, level of pay, quality of communication, tools, equipment, materials, physical work conditions, employee selection and placement, and many others. However, there are three factors that you should make a special effort to remember.

First, there must be a good person to job match. Performance is affected by the fit or match between the employee and the job. If an employee's interests, aptitude and ability are not congruent with the nature of his or her job or with the environment within which the job is performed, then performance at the desired levels will most likely not be achieved. If there is a good person to job match then performance can be optimized.

Key Point
In order for work performance to be optimized there must be a good person to job match.

Next, an employee must know exactly what is expected of him or her on the job. Not just what the nature of the job is but also how fast it must be done, to what quality levels, what deadlines are set and much more. Lastly, even when clear quantitative and qualitative job standards are set, it is important that employees know exactly how well they are meeting those standards. This is the process of feedback or performance appraisal.

Most organizations have formal performance appraisal or review systems. Your organization probably has one, too. Effective performance appraisal is much more than a once-a-year activity. It is also more than just an evaluative process. Performance appraisal is equally evaluative and developmental. It is also an on-going process involving day-to-day contact between the supervisor and subordinate.

Key Point
Performance appraisal is an on-going process that is both evaluative and developmental.

Often we think of job performance standards as being set mainly for factory jobs and then through industrial engineering methods. Many work standards are set using time measurement methods like MTM. However, there are other ways to establish job standards and many of these are just as suitable for office work as they are for industrial jobs.

One way that you can set work standards for employees is through the use of historical data and through your own experience. Historical data is that which is available through a study of past records. The records should be detailed enough to provide information like how many claims per hour a claims adjuster can handle; or what the average response time is to customer inquiries. Once this information is available it is possible to determine the work load that an average person under normal conditions can handle.

Many supervisors have been promoted to their current positions from the ranks of those who they now supervise. This usually means that at one time they probably performed the same work that their subordinates now perform. If this is case you can compare the quantity and quality standards that you met with what your employees are now achieving. If you did not previously do work similar to that of your subordinates then try to identify (1) an average employee, (2) a superior employee and (3) a below average employee, if any, among the employees in your work group. The relative performance of these employees will serve as a guideline or benchmark which will help you to set work group performance standards.

Key Point
One of the best ways to establish meaningful job performance standards is through employee involvement.

If you have already succeeded in building an effective team and in creating an empowered climate then the best and most practical way to set work standards is to involve your subordinates in setting them. This might seem difficult but most employees have a very positive attitude toward work and work output. The experience of most managers, supervisors and other work group leaders who have tried this method clearly shows that when involved, the majority of employees actually set standards higher than those set by their superiors. Here is how you can work with the members of your work group to set meaningful job standards.

1. Explain that work standards are a way of ensuring that everyone has a clear understanding of what is expected of them and of the company's performance goals.

2. Ask the employees to identify the key components of their jobs.

3. Have the employees break the major components of their jobs into specific tasks or elements.

4. Ask them to write a performance standard for each key task or element. A performance standard can be defined as a condition that will exist when the job has been satisfactorily performed.

5. If the goal or standard suggested by the employee is below what you believe is reasonable, then discuss the standard with him or her and find out the reason for the difference. Try to reach a consensus decision on an appropriate standard.

Key Point
When analyzing performance problems first determine if the problem is caused by a skill deficiency.

Being able to determine why an employee is not performing up to standard and knowing the most effective corrective action to take is a very important responsibility of any manager, supervisor or other work group leader. One of the best methods for doing this is to first carefully identify the specific performance problem that the employee is having. Next, determine if it is a skill or non-skill deficiency.

A skill deficiency usually exists when the employee either does not know how to do the job or lacks proficiency doing it. Non-skill deficiencies cover all other possible causes of non-performance. If the performance problem is caused by a skill deficiency make sure that the employee knows and understands the job methods and has received sufficient recent training. If it is caused by a non-skill deficiency look for motivational barriers or barriers caused by organizational problems like poor communication, poor job design and poor quality equipment or material. Be sure to seek out problem root causes not simply symptoms.

From time to time, no matter how positive your approach or how rational your method might be, you might experience failure and frustration trying to correct employee performance problems. If this happens you may have to take disciplinary action. The basic objective of discipline is to ensure conformance with established policies, procedures and work rules. In principle discipline is not punitive. It is an action which is part of the controlling function of the management cycle; action taken to eliminate any negative variance between what should be and what is.

Discipline is morale building. Studies have clearly shown that the majority of employees in most organizations expect their supervisors to take corrective action with those employees whose performance or behavior does not conform with the standards being met by other employees.

Key Point
When employee discipline is required be fair, decisive and follow the principle of progressive discipline.

If discipline is required you must be fair, decisive and follow the practice of progressive discipline. Progressive discipline means administering moderate discipline for a first disciplinary occasion and, then, if the employee fails to improve, increasing the measure of discipline applied.

1. For performance problems, the following steps are suggested when discipline is necessary:

2. Meet with the employee in private. Maintain your own composure and maintain respect for the employee's personal dignity.

3. Begin the meeting by reviewing any previous counseling sessions that you have had with the employee about the problem.

4. Be specific about the standard that the employee is expected to meet and about the actual performance of the employee.

5. Ask the employee why the deficiency exists and what he or she can do to correct the problem.

6. State your own plan of action for the employee if it is more effective than the employee's plan.

7. If the employee has been counseled about the problem before and has failed to respond then administer whatever disciplinary action is appropriate for the infraction.

8. Express confidence that the employee can and will improve. Point out that failure to improve will result in more severe discipline.

The administration of a penalty, whether to correct conduct or other work performance problems, should always be your last resort. First make every reasonable effort to improve the employee's performance through coaching, counseling and other methods. But, if it does become necessary, then administer discipline decisively. You will be respected by your employees for doing so.

Summary

As a supervisor, it is your responsibility to ensure that the quality and output of your work unit is fully meeting the expectations of your superiors. In order to do this, you must ensure that each of your subordinates is doing his or her fair share and is meeting established job performance standards.

Employee work performance is influenced by many factors. However, ultimately performance is determined by the motivation, skill, and ability of the individual employee to perform a job. In addition to these requisites employees must know what is expected of them on the job in quantitative and qualitative terms. They must also know how well they are meeting those expectations.

Performance standards are essential to successful job performance. Without standards it is difficult for employees to have a clear understanding of their supervisor's expectations. Time measurement, historical data, personal experience of the supervisor and employee involvement are among the many ways by which work standards are set.

Performance appraisal, feedback, coaching and counseling are important tools for maintaining and improving employee work performance. When dealing with a performance problem, first determine if it is a skill or non-skill deficiency and then develop appropriate alternative remedies. The administration of employee discipline may be necessary in order to deal with persistent performance problems. When this is required it should be administered fairly, consistently, progressively and decisively.

Improving Employee Work Performance Self-Awareness Test

Instructions: Decide whether each of the statements below is true **(T)**, false **(F)** or whether you are uncertain **(?)** about it. Indicate your decision by placing a mark in the appropriate column to the right of each statement.

		T	?	F
01.	Ability, skill and motivation have a greater affect on job performance than do supervisory practices.	☐	☐	☐
02.	Ability is a person's physical, intellectual and psychological capability.	☐	☐	☐
03.	Job standards are more suitable in some organizations than in others.	☐	☐	☐
04.	Employees cannot perform effectively unless they have sufficient feedback about their performance.	☐	☐	☐
05.	Job design, training and the quality of materials and equipment affect performance but not motivation.	☐	☐	☐
06.	The main objective of a performance appraisal interview is to evaluate employee performance.	☐	☐	☐
07.	Most employees dislike job performance standards.	☐	☐	☐
08.	Performance problems can usually be corrected by disciplining an employee.	☐	☐	☐
09.	Discipline is a negative action and should only be used as a last resort.	☐	☐	☐
10.	When disciplining an employee the focus should be on the "record" and not on the employee personally.	☐	☐	☐

Personal Developmental Plan

Prepare a development plan to improve your performance management skills by answering the following questions.

A. The performance management skills that I use most frequently and that are currently my greatest strengths are:

B. The performance management skills in which I currently need the greatest improvement are:

C. My personal objectives for improving my performance management skills are:

D. The specific strategies by which I plan to develop and strengthen my performance management skills are (use additional paper if necessary):

1.

2.

3.

4.

5.

Chapter 10
Coaching And Counseling

Learning Objectives

After completing this chapter you will have learned:

The difference between the skills of coaching and counseling.

How to conduct a productive counseling session that resolves employees' concerns, problems or complaints.

How to conduct a constructive coaching session that improves employee job performance.

A few years ago a major university conducted a study to determine what distinguished effective supervisors from those who were less successful. Thousands of employees in many different businesses, industrial and governmental organizations were surveyed as part of this study. The consensus of these employees can be summarized as follows:

"I like my supervisor; he (she) listens to me."

One of the most important skills that a manager, supervisor or other work group leader can acquire is the skill to listen to employees effectively, specifically, the skill of **active listening**.

The skill of active listening was discussed in an earlier chapter of this book. Its relevance to this chapter is that the willingness and ability to listen to employees concerns, problems and complaints is the foundation of two additional skills, coaching and counseling.

Although similar, there is a difference between the two skills. Employees are counseled about their job related concerns, problems and complaints. They are coached about ways to improve work performance. Both coaching and counseling can be developmental. However, only coaching directly confronts employees about the record of their job performance.

Key Point
The skill of coaching directly confronts employees about the record of their job performance.

At one time or another almost everyone has had a concern about a job related matter, made a complaint to his or her supervisor or has had a job related problem. Complaints are very important aspects of the communication process. Quite contrary to some lines of thinking, things are not always better when it is quiet in the shop or office. Often the absence of complaints signals serious obstacles in the communication process; such as lack of approachability on the part of the work group leader, lack of trust, feelings of restriction on speaking up and telling it like it is, or the existence of unproductive conflict.

Key Point
The absence of complaints from employees can indicate serious obstacles in the communication process.

For example, even if the concerns, problems and complaints of employees were suppressed, annoyances and irritants would still exist. Without an outlet they would build up. Problems would not get resolved. Performance, productivity, and quality would drop. Mistrust and suspicion would cause poor interpersonal relationships. A very unproductive situation would certainly exist. On the other hand, the supervisory practice of counseling enables employees to express their concerns, problems and complaints. It builds trust, empowerment and it contributes to improved supervisor - employee communication.

Active listening skills are essential in order to effectively counsel an employee about a concern, problem or complaint. Employees are not always able to express themselves accurately. An employee may complain about one thing while he or she is really bothered by something else. For example, an employee may complain about pay or a work assignment while the real problem is her belief that the quality of his work is not recognized. In most cases the employee is not trying to withhold anything. Rather, she may not really understand the basis for her feeling of dissatisfaction. When this occurs the skill of active listening is needed in order to identify the problem root cause; to separate the wheat from the chaff.

Key Point
Whether or not a supervisor believes that an employee's complaint has merit, it is important to the employee.

One thing that you should always keep in mind is that whether or not you personally think that the problem or complaint is important or legitimate, the chances are that the employee does! If you pay little attention to it, demean or belittle it, or show annoyance or irritation at being bothered, then in a very real way you are "putting down" something of value and importance to your employee. You should also keep in mind that it might have taken a considerable amount of courage for the employee to speak up. Sometimes managers and supervisors do not fully appreciate the power of their position as perceived by employees. Even though you might try to be friendly and approachable, some employees may feel uncomfortable or even embarrassed coming to you with their problems. Here are seven steps that will help you to effectively counsel and help employees who are dissatisfied with certain job related conditions or who need your help to resolve a job related problem or concern.

1. Be Friendly and Approachable

Counseling employees about complaints, grievances and problems is one of the most important of your many responsibilities. In order to fulfill this responsibility, employees must feel comfortable approaching you. Projecting a helpful attitude and making it clear that you are willing to meet with them will go a long way to establish your approachability. This does not mean that you must drop everything the moment an employee asks to see you. No, but it does mean that you should avoid unnecessary delays arranging the meeting and that you should hold it as soon as possible.

2. Meet in Private

Whatever the nature of the employee's complaint or problem, it should not be aired in public. This is a matter to be discussed between you and the employee. Arrange for a private place to discuss it.

Key Point
The more you show a willingness to listen, the greater the chances the employee will "open up."

3. Listen, Listen, Listen

Apply your active listening skill. The more you show a willingness to listen, the greater the chances that your subordinates will "open up." The more they open up, the better your chances are of getting to the root cause of the issue or problem.

4. Determine the Real Issue

Use your active listening skills to identify the real problem and its root cause. Often the apparent problem is just a surface issue. For example, an employee who complains about money or a work assignment may actually be concerned about lack of recognition.

5. Ask for the Employee's Suggestions

In many cases, the employee will simply be ventilating or trying to get something off his or her chest. Just listening will be helpful. However, in most cases, the complaint or problem must be resolved.

One way to begin this process is to ask the employee for his or her suggestions about what should be done to resolve the matter. In many cases, talking the matter out and being asked to come up with a solution truly helps to quickly resolve the whole matter. Then too, the employee might have an idea that is fully workable.

6. **Be Fair, Uniform and Consistent**

   Few things contribute to employee relations problems as much as actual or perceived unfair or biased treatment. When you make your decision and take responsive action about an employee's complaint, concern or problem it is essential to be uniform and consistent with how similar issues or problems have been settled. Under no circumstance is bias or prejudice acceptable in the way employees are treated or in the way their skills are used.

7. **Think and Decide**

   Be decisive, but don't be pressed into making a spot decision if one is not absolutely necessary. Study the merits of the issue or problem carefully. Make sure that you have gathered all of the facts. Include in your study all relevant company policies, procedures and work rules together with a review of past practice. Then decide and inform the employee of your decision.

Coaching is a companion skill to counseling, but unlike the latter coaching focuses on job performance. Coaching is almost always initiated by the manager, supervisor or other work group leader rather than by the employee. During the coaching meeting or interview the focus is on the employee's job performance record. Opportunities for the employee to improve or to excel in his or her job performance are explored. Job performance deficiencies are openly and candidly confronted and discussed. In this way coaching is both evaluative and developmental.

Key Point
Coaching employees in ways to improve their job performance should be a regular part of a supervisor's planned activities.

Coaching employees in ways by which they can improve their job performance should be a regular part of a supervisor's planned work activities. It should be an on-going process consistent with the total quality management concept of continuous improvement. Here are some guidelines for conducting a successful coaching meeting with subordinates.

1. **Review the Purpose and Objectives of the Meeting**
Inform the employee that the purpose of the meeting is to review the employee's performance record in relation to job standards. Stress the developmental benefits that can accrue from the meeting and express your interest in using the meeting as an additional opportunity for both parties to discuss job related matters of mutual interest.

Key Point
Studies have shown that in most cases employees tend to be objective about the quality of their job performance.

2. **Ask the Employee for His or Her Self Appraisal.**

    Ask the employee to state the performance standards for his or her job. Then ask the employee for a self-appraisal regarding how well those standards are being met. Use your listening skills. This is a good way to quickly promote a constructive discussion. The chances are that your subordinate will feel more comfortable and less threatened if he or she tells you how well his or her performance matched the work standard rather that have you do so. Studies have shown that in most cases when employees are asked for self appraisals they tend to be objective about the quality of their job performance -- even to the point of often being more critical than their superiors.

3. **Seek Out Causes for Performance Variances**

    If a performance deficiency exists it will not be corrected until both you and the employee identify the problem root cause. Only then will you be able to develop appropriate corrective action. However, you should be just as interested in learning what the employee is doing to achieve above average performance on any aspect of the job. That way you can help the employee identify behaviors that are contributing to success and possibly train other employees in these positive behaviors.

4. Inform the Employee of Your Own Assessment.

In the final analysis your own judgment, modified if appropriate by any new inputs from the employee, must be the governing factor. If you are using objective, documented, job-related performance measurement criteria, then subject to the possibility of honest error your assessment must prevail. If the employee's self appraisal has not covered all of the issues completely or accurately, then you must do so now.

5. Develop Remedial Strategies

Performance studies in most organizations show that the vast majority of employees perform at least at a satisfactory level. Because of this, even when an employee has certain performance deficiencies it is likely that some parts of his or her job are being performed satisfactorily. Recognize any positive work behaviors and ask the employee what action he or she can take to correct performance deficiencies.

If the employee has no suggestion for ways to improve or if you do not believe that the suggested strategies will be effective then present your own performance improvement strategies. Be specific and set measurable, realistic goals together a plan for accomplishing the goals.

6. Discuss Additional Job-Related Subjects

Take full advantage of this opportunity to discuss other job related matters of mutual interest or concern with the employee. Avoid "small talk" and non-job related, personal matters. Use this occasion to reinforce your ongoing willingness to listen to the employee and to be a coach, helper, and facilitator. Be sure to learn if the employee needs any special help or support from you in order to successfully accomplish the performance improvement objectives that were set.

7. **Summarize, Arrange for Follow-Up and Close**

   Recap the main points covered during the meeting, including any action plans. Agree on what follow-up should be taken and when it will be done. Then, close the meeting on a friendly, positive note.

Some managers, supervisors or other work group leaders may think that the above steps are easy to master. However, a study by the Conference Board, a national research organization, showed that only about 10% of all managers and supervisors were skilled in conducting performance related interviews with employees. Clearly, this is a skill that requires considerable effort and practice in order to achieve the necessary level of proficiency. But it is a very crucial skill that all managers, supervisors and other work group leaders must acquire and regularly use.

During a coaching interview the focus should be on the job performance record and not on less subjective criteria. Variances from job standard should be identified, causes determined and remedial action plans, including the employee's own improvement strategies, should be developed.

Summary

The skills of coaching and counseling are crucial responsibilities of all managers, supervisors and other work group leaders. Counseling relates to the supervisory practice of actively listening and responding to employee complaints, grievances and problems; all of which represent a way for employees to express matters of concern to their superiors. As a manager, supervisor or other work group leader one of your major responsibilities is to counsel employees about these matters. Failure to properly counsel employees about issues or problems of concern to them can result in lower morale and productivity, poor quality and higher costs.

The most effective complaint, grievance or problem counselors are those who convey a sincere impression of friendliness and approachability, who meet with employees in private, listen carefully, ask employees for their suggestions, ensure fairness and uniformity and then make their own decision after careful study.

Coaching refers to the practice of confronting an employee about job performance with the objective of finding ways to overcome deficiencies and improve job performance. Because coaching is both evaluative and developmental it can motivate employees to achieve peak performance.

Coaching And Counseling Self-Awareness Test

Instructions: Decide whether each of the statements below is true **(T)**, false **(F)** or whether you are uncertain **(?)** about it. Indicate your decision by placing a mark in the appropriate column to the right of each statement.

		T	?	F
01.	Coaching and counseling have the same purpose.	☐	☐	☐
02.	The most important skill needed to conduct a counseling session is the skill of active listening.	☐	☐	☐
03	Both coaching and counseling should be used to confront employees about performance problems.	☐	☐	☐
04.	A good way to judge leadership effectiveness is by the absence of complaints.	☐	☐	☐
05.	Coaching is evaluative -- not developmental.	☐	☐	☐
06.	The perceived power of a leader's position may affect his or her approachability.	☐	☐	☐
07.	Coaching sessions should begin with "small talk" to help relax an employee.	☐	☐	☐
08.	Very few employees can be relied on to objectively evaluate their own job performance.	☐	☐	☐
09.	Only about 10% of all managers and supervisors are skilled in the practice of coaching.	☐	☐	☐
10.	In a coaching session, a supervisor should ask employees what their suggestions are for ways to improve their job performance.	☐	☐	☐

Personal Developmental Plan

Prepare a development plan to improve your coaching and counseling skills by answering the following questions.

A. The coaching and counseling skills that I use most frequently and that are currently my greatest strengths are:

B. The coaching and counseling skills in which I currently need the greatest improvement are:

C. My personal objectives for improving my coaching and counseling skills are:

D. The specific strategies by which I plan to develop and strengthen my coaching and counseling skills are (use additional paper if necessary):

    1.

    2.

    3.

    4.

    5.

Chapter 11
Managing Cultural Diversity

> ## Learning Objectives
>
> **After completing this chapter you will have learned:**
>
> Why inter-cultural communication skill is important to your role as a leader.
>
> How misunderstandings can arise among culturally diverse employees.
>
> How you can improve communication and relationships with employees of different cultural backgrounds.

Government data indicates that women, minorities and people from other countries now comprise about 70 percent of the American work force. The reports further states that within a few more years this figure will increase to 80 percent or more. This means that most managers, supervisors and other leaders are either now dealing with a culturally diverse work force or they soon will be!

Key Point
About seventy percent of today's work force is comprised of culturally diverse employees.

Cultural diversity offers incredible opportunity for individuals to learn, grow and gain enriching personal and professional experiences. But, at the same time it presents one of the greatest challenges of our time. A challenge, which if not properly met, can lead to cultural shock and its very real physical symptoms: disorientation, insomnia, eating disorders, anxiety, depression and identity crisis.

At the heart of cultural diversity is a set of interpersonal interactions between people of different cultures; Asians, Blacks, Arabs, Hispanics, Native Americans, Europeans -- men and women of different cultures who do not necessarily share a common heritage, common traditions, customs, values or language. In most cases these interactions are constructive. However, inter-cultural interaction problems can occur when people of one culture misunderstand or misinterpret the behaviors of people of a different culture. In most cases the cause of the misunderstanding or misinterpretation can be traced to verbal and non-verbal communication distortions

It would be simplistic to suggest that communication distortions are the only causes of conflict between people of different cultures. Some biases and prejudices are very deeply rooted in the historical relationships of various cultural groups. However, on a practical level, the cultural diversity management issues which confront most leaders in business, industry and government are communication related. Because of this it is important that managers, supervisors and other leaders not only increase their inter-cultural awareness and sensitivity and also improve their inter-cultural communication skills as well.

The term culture is applied to a variety of situations. It is used to distinguish the way people in one country live from the way people in other countries live. In some cases it is used to distinguish between two or more levels of technological sophistication; e.g. an advanced culture versus a primitive culture. Culture is also used to identify the social attributes and characteristics of an entire organization or of a group of people within an organization.

Key Point
Culture is a set of behaviors, perceptions, attitudes and beliefs that are affected by a group's social norms.

What is culture and how does it affect people in business, industry and government? Culture is a set of behaviors, a way of thinking, perceptions, attitudes and beliefs that are affected by the social norms and values of a group of people. Culture affects all people in all countries and sectors of the world. It influences what they wear, eat and drink and their appearance. It also influences their perception of others and the world around them (their environment), what and how they communicate and it affects the way they interact both with each other and with strangers or people from other cultures.

For example, in some cultures people tend to rigidly follow time schedules and, when engaged in business, become upset if they are late for an appointment. In other cultures, like Latin cultures, people take a more relaxed view of time. In these cultures it is customary for meetings to begin a half hour or more after they are scheduled and it is often expected for the boss to arrive even later.

Another example of a cultural difference is the practice in many western countries of recognizing and praising the accomplishment of individual employees which differs from the focus of some eastern cultures that place more emphasis on the accomplishments of teams or groups of employees, instead.

Key Point
Culture provides individuals and groups of individuals with an essential sense of identity.

Culture provides individuals and groups of individuals with an essential sense of identity. It provides them with a model of social behaviors, norms and values which when followed offer the means by which people can gain social acceptance. At the same time, a tendency to focus inward on one's own culture only can lead to a condition of ethnocentrism in which people lack sensitivity to other cultures and tend to judge other cultures by their own values and norms. This can have unfortunate consequences whenever it happens. However, in the work place a tendency to judge others only by the values and standards of one's own culture can have a very serious negative affect on morale, interpersonal relationships, quality and productivity.

Throughout history there has been conflict between people of different cultures. Many of these conflicts have their origins in ancient animosities, including historical conflict among religious sects, that have since become obscure yet still endure. Others are caused by common human failings like greed, the drive for power and wealth and a disregard for human values – a condition so sadly still apparent in the present time. Conflict also exists between people of different cultures who share the same community and work place. In some cases the causes of this conflict are similar to those described above. However, much more commonly inter-cultural conflict among community members and fellow employees can be traced to two communication related causes: (1) a lack understanding by people of one culture about the people of a different culture, and (2) misinterpretations and distortions that occur when people of different cultures communicate with each other.

Key Point
Most inter-cultural problems are caused by communication distortions and misinterpretations.

Because people of one culture generally share common values, traditions, customs and other social norms they tend to perceive people of a different culture as "strangers." Strangers, at least initially, are viewed with caution and their ways (culture) may not be understood. Major problems can develop when the people of one culture are unable or unwilling to understand cultural differences in communication, practices and thought patterns among those who they view as being strangers. The result can be cultural shock with serious and very real symptoms like disorientation, sleeping and eating disorders, anxiety and depression.

Key Point
Language, thought processes, non-verbal behavior, values and norms are factors that affect inter-cultural communication.

Social scientists have identified several important factors that affect communication and understanding among people of different cultures.

Language

The inability of one culture to understand another and the possibility of misinterpretation obviously increases when the parties do not share a common language. However, even when the parties speak the same language understanding and interpretation problems can still exist because of accent, nuances, vocabulary and translation errors. One party might interpret a heavy foreign accent to mean that the speaker does not have a good command of the former's language (not at all necessarily true), for instance. Or, the wrong word, correctly pronounced, might convey a greatly different message than the speaker intended.

Thought Processes

What people think and believe and how they form their perceptions can have a significant affect on communication and understanding. Religious beliefs, ethnic traditions and customs, attitudes toward gender relationships, and economic status are examples of only a few of these social factors. A thought process called contexting, however, can have a particularly important impact on inter-cultural communication.

Contexting is the extent that a communication sender and receiver share a common understanding of the meaning and implication of what is communicated within the circumstances influenced by their particular culture. In some cultures the true essence of a message is communicated not by what is said but by how it is said or by what is omitted. The more communicators share a common understanding of the message context the less they need to say in words or gestures.

Most North Americans are low context communicators and, therefore, need to communicate with each other in a precise, literal way. People of most Eastern and Mid-Eastern cultures are high context communicators who do not need to be as explicit to be understood. Many inter-cultural relationship problems arise because of contexting misinterpretations.

Non-Verbal Behavior

It is estimated that about 65% of a message's meaning is communicated through body language. Gestures, signs, symbols, touching and even the space between face-to-face communicators have all been found to have a major affect on understanding. Unfortunately, the meaning conveyed through non-verbal communication differs greatly among cultures and has the potential to cause serious misinterpretation problems. For example, in some cultures the traditional North American signal meaning "OK" (fingers formed in a ring) is considered to be an obscene gesture. A nod of the head that signifies understanding or agreement in one culture can simply be a face saving gesture in another culture. Standing practically "nose-to-nose" when communicating face-to-face may be the norm in one culture but can be considered an invasion of privacy in another. Lack of sensitivity and awareness about alternative cultural meanings of non-verbal communication behavior can result in unwanted and unnecessary inter-cultural misunderstandings.

Values and Norms

The values and norms of a culture are often shaped by historical events, economic conditions and status, social roles and similar factors. Economically disadvantaged groups, for example, may develop a set of attitudes and beliefs which are considerably different from those held by people of more affluent groups in the same country or even the same community. This condition has led to the rise of subcultures or micro cultures that exist concurrently within a larger society (a macro culture).

Religious, racial, ethnic, gender and other micro cultures exist within most North American business, industrial and governmental organizations. Not only have many of these micro cultures developed their own sets of social values and norms, but many are also characterized by distinctive thought process patterns like contexting and by language differentials. In order for you to effectively fulfill your role as a leader within your organization you must learn, understand and be responsive to these cultural differences that might exist among the employees in your work group.

Key Point
Inter-cultural communication can be improved through awareness, understanding, active listening and feedback.

Here are several action steps that you can take to improve your inter-cultural communication skills and, as a result, improve your ability to more effectively manage cultural diversity:

1. **Awareness:** Increase your awareness and sensitivity about the composition of employees within your work group, especially with respect to any cultural differences that might exist. Be sensitive to the fact that the perceptions of these employees about their jobs, the work environment and their relationships with both you and their coworkers may differ from the perceptions of others.

2. **Understanding:** Learn about the culture of those employees whose culture differs from your own. Ask them questions about it. Show interest, understanding and empathy. Build trust with them so that minor mistakes and misinterpretations do not develop into major problems.

3. **Active Listening:** Your listening skills are particularly important when dealing with employees of other cultures. Active listening means listening non-judgmentally and responding in a way that encourages further communication from the message sender. In addition, learn as much as you can about the contexting within the employee's culture. This will further help to avoid misinterpretations.

4. **Feedback:** Recognize the North American tendency to communicate in a low context manner while other cultures may be high context communicators. Be precise in your communication with employees of other cultures and do not expect them to necessarily interpret things the way you do. Provide the speaker with feedback in the form of restating what he or she said in order to ensure understanding. Similarly, ask the employee to restate your message to him or her.

Summary

The work force of this century and beyond has become and will continue to be highly culturally diversified. It is estimated that in the near future as much as 80 percent of the American work force will be comprised of people from other countries, women and minorities. This diversity of cultures offers both challenges and opportunities for all employees but especially for managers, supervisors and other leaders of organizations. The term culture refers to a set of behaviors, a way of thinking, perceptions, attitudes and beliefs that are affected by the social norms and values of a group of people. The culture of one group of people affects their interaction with people of other cultures. Inter-cultural problems can occur when people of one culture interpret the behavior of other cultures by their own standards, values and norms.

Most inter-cultural problems in business, industry and government are caused by communication distortions and misinterpretations. Among the factors affecting inter-cultural communication are language, thought processes, non-verbal behavior, values and norms. Managers, supervisors and other leaders can improve their inter-cultural communication skills and, as a result, improve their ability to more effectively manage a culturally diverse work force by using the four-step process of awareness, understanding, active listening and feedback.

Managing Cultural Diversity Self-Awareness Test

Instructions: Decide whether each of the statements below is true **(T)**, false **(F)** or whether you are uncertain **(?)** about it. Indicate your decision by placing a mark in the appropriate column to the right of each statement.

		T	?	F
01.	Culturally diverse employees are the slowest growing segment of the American work force.	☐	☐	☐
02.	A strong foreign accent usually indicates that the speaker lacks a good understanding of English.	☐	☐	☐
03.	Non-verbal communication like gestures and facial expressions means the same thing worldwide.	☐	☐	☐
04.	Thought patterns, reasoning and logic occur the same way among all cultures.	☐	☐	☐
05.	Culturally diverse employees should be persuaded to quickly adopt North American values and norms.	☐	☐	☐
06.	Culturally diverse employees almost always respond accurately to precise, direct questions.	☐	☐	☐
07.	The quality of a culture can be judged by its technological sophistication.	☐	☐	☐
08.	The American communication culture is high context.	☐	☐	☐
09.	Praising the achievements of individuals is a management practice that is common among all cultures.	☐	☐	☐
10.	Little of a message's meaning is conveyed through non-verbal behavior.	☐	☐	☐

Personal Developmental Plan

Prepare a development plan to improve your diversity management skills by answering the following questions.

A. The diversity management skills that I use most frequently and that are currently my greatest strengths are:

B. The diversity management skills in which I currently need the greatest improvement are:

C. My personal objectives for improving my diversity management skills are:

D. The specific strategies by which I plan to develop and strengthen my diversity management skills are (use additional paper if necessary):

1.

2.

3.

4.

5.

Chapter 12
Focusing On Total Quality

> ## Learning Objectives
> **After completing this chapter you will have learned:**
>
> The history and importance of today's nation-wide movement to improve product and service quality.
>
> The definition and key principles of total quality management (TQM).
>
> What you can do to establish a total quality climate within your own work group.

During the past several years a new quality consciousness has been sweeping through North American industrial, service and governmental organizations. The focus of this consciousness is the need to meet the challenges of foreign competition by improving productivity and product and service quality. The term "Total Quality Management" (TQM) is widely used to describe the processes and systems used by organizations to effect these necessary improvements.

TQM is one of the most important management concepts to be introduced to the work place in the past several decades. As a manager, supervisor or other organizational leader you have an important responsibility to understand the importance of this movement, its background and history and to learn what you can do to help your work group achieve total quality performance.

Key Point

As a leader in your organization you have a responsibility to learn what you can do to help your work group achieve total quality performance.

The total quality movement is an effort to reestablish a priority on quality performance in this country. However, prior to World War II, and for several years thereafter, the United States enjoyed pre-eminence as the leading industrial power in the world. During this period the quality of American made products was matched only by the pride and craftsmanship of American workers and the pride that was taken in the "Made in America" label. Unfortunately, during the cultural revolution of the 1960s and 1970s America lost considerable ground in both the productivity of its workforce and in the quality of its products and services.

Key Point
During the cultural revolution of the 1960s and 1970s America lost considerable ground in both the productivity of its workforce and in the quality of its products.

In more recent years the American economy has reeled under a relentless attack by foreign competition. An attack that has resulted in the loss of hundreds of thousands of jobs (many exported to countries like India, Indonesia, Bangladesh and now China), high unemployment, a steady reduction in the quality of life for millions of people. One example will be found in the auto industry where in the period from 1980 through 2000 Japanese auto manufacturers like Honda and Toyota supplanted American auto companies with respect to both market share and also product quality; a condition that only in very recent years has shown signs of a possible reversal

Key Point
Dr. W. Edwards Deming's 14 points for total quality improvement serve as the basis for Japan's success in producing high quality products.

Ironically, Japan's competitive edge was gained, in part, because Japanese business executives were willing to listen to the message of an American quality expert, Dr. W. Edwards Deming. In the late 1950's Deming traveled to Japan, as the guest of the Japanese Union of Scientists and Engineers (JUSE), to help rebuild Japan's devastated war economy. He did this by giving quality improvement lectures to executives, engineers and managers. Deming focused his message on statistical quality control and his now famous 14 Points for total quality improvement.

Although Deming's ideas were widely and enthusiastically embraced in Japan, they fell on deaf ears in the United States. Fortunately, since that time a collective concern for quality has arisen throughout America. Faced with damaging foreign competition and a battered economy, leaders in business, industry and government finally began to listen to Dr. Deming and to other prestigious quality authorities like Joseph M. Juran and Philip B. Crosby. Then, in 1982 Congress passed legislation for the formation of a national conference to address the issue of declining productivity and quality. From this was born the Malcolm Baldrige National Quality Improvement Act (1987) and the subsequent establishment of the Malcolm Baldrige National Quality Award (named after the late U.S. Secretary of Commerce).

Key Point
The Malcolm Baldrige National Quality Award is presented each year to organizations that meet demanding quality performance standards.

The Malcolm Baldrige National Quality Award is now presented each year to organizations that meet demanding performance criteria in seven focal areas: leadership, information and analysis, strategic quality planning, human resource utilization, quality assurance, quality assurance results, and customer satisfaction. Most, but not all, of these criteria are shared by the Deming philosophy. What is shared in common are these essential concepts:

- Total quality means fully meeting customer (internal and external) needs and expectations.

- Total quality is the key to superior organization performance.

- Superior organization performance is essential to organizational profitability and survivability.

- Total quality can only be achieved through a collaborative process of commitment, teamwork, and problem solving guided by the proactive leadership of top management.

- Total quality is a continuous process that is dependent upon effective human resource utilization including work force education, training, skill development and the sharing of appropriate rewards for the achievement of success.

- Each member of the organization, at whatever level, is personally responsible for achieving total quality with respect to the product or service he or she produces.

Key Point
The most widely accepted definition of the term "total quality" is fully meeting customers needs and expectations.

This criterion is now widely accepted as the definition of total quality. Ensuring that this is accomplished is total quality management. A more recent modification of the original TQM philosophy is an approach called Six Sigma, a process improvement methodology. Six Sigma originated in 1986 as a result of Motorola's drive towards reducing defects by minimizing process variation.. The main difference between TQM and Six Sigma is the approach. TQM tries to improve quality by ensuring conformance to internal requirements, while Six Sigma focuses on improving quality by reducing the number of defects. Also, during the past number of years a family of quality standards called ISO 9000 (and now its successor ISO 14,000) has been established by the International Organization for Standardization in Geneva,

Switzerland. These standards have now been widely accepted throughout industry in almost all industrialized countries. Six Sigma and the ISO standards fully embrace the principles of TQM and so they are complementary to TQM rather than being a replacement for it.

Implementing a total quality management program throughout an entire organization is a very big job. It begins with top management's commitment and continues with extensive planning, analysis, resource organization, climate setting, training and a lot more. It may take several months just to plan for a TQM program in a medium size company and even longer to develop the climate conditions necessary for success. But, there is a lot that you can do to ensure total quality performance by all of the employees in your work group. Here are some steps that you can take right now to exercise total quality leadership:

1. **Commit To Total Quality** -- Make a personal commitment to totally meet the needs and expectations of your work group customers (internal customers like other departments or work groups as well as any outside customers). You must then clearly communicate this commitment to all of the employees in your work group and obtain their individual commitment to the same goal.

2. **Build A Team** -- Teamwork and collaboration are essential to achieving total quality. The subject of teamwork is covered elsewhere in this program and includes important techniques like empowerment practices, developing and open communication system, involving employees in problem solving and more.

3. **Evaluate And Analyze Your Work Group's Performance** -- Product and service quality cannot be ensured nor can improvement begin until you have an accurate process to measure the performance of your work group. Learn how to use data collection methods and statistical techniques like Pareto Analysis, Histograms and control charts to identify <u>and prevent</u> variance from quality standards. These methods are fully suitable for both factory (plant) and office work procedures.

4. **Focus On Prevention** -- Dedicate yourself and your work group to doing it right the first time. Look for ways to **prevent** quality problems from happening rather than spending a lot of time, money and effort to fix problems after they occur.

5. **Strive For Continuous Improvement** -- Adopt the philosophy that there is always a better way to do it; that improvement is always possible. Involve your employees in looking for a better way and encourage them to be creative and innovative. Continuous improvement also applies to further developing your own job skills and those of the members of your work group.

6. **Share Responsibility, Recognition And Rewards** -- You can't do it alone. Total quality performance is a collaborative team effort on the part of all of the members of your work group. You must ensure that each member of your work group shares responsibility for producing a high quality product or service. It also means that recognition and rewards for achieving desired results are shared by all those who contributed to the effort.

Summary

The need to meet the challenges of foreign competition together with a renewed consciousness about the importance of product and service quality has given rise to a nation-wide movement called Total Quality Management (TQM). TQM is a term that is used to describe the technical and human systems and processes used by business, industrial and governmental organizations to ensure that their products and services fully meet their customers' needs and expectations.

TQM is based on quality improvement principles advocated by Dr. W. Edwards Deming, Joseph M. Juran, Philip B. Crosby and other experts in quality management methods and systems. In 1987 the philosophy and many of the principles developed by these experts were embodied in the Malcolm Baldrige National Quality Improvement Act and in the subsequent establishment of the Malcolm Baldrige National Quality Award, a prestigious award granted annually to those organizations that meet exacting quality criteria.

TQM can only be achieved through a collaborative process of commitment, teamwork, continuous improvement, including continuous employee training and skill development, and systematic problem solving. Although implementing a full TQM program in an organization is a major undertaking, there are several things that each manager, supervisor or other work group leader can do **now** to exercise total quality leadership within his or her work group. Among them are the following:

1. Making a personal commitment to total quality,
2. Building an effective work team,
3. Evaluating work group performance,
4. Focusing on prevention,
5. Striving for continuous improvement, and
6. Sharing responsibility, recognition and rewards.

The product of these strategies will be significantly improved work group performance and the achievement of TQM's overall objective; fully meeting customers' needs and expectations.

Focusing On Total Quality Awareness Test

Instructions: Decide whether each of the statements below is true **(T)**, false **(F)** or whether you are uncertain **(?)** about it. Indicate your decision by placing a mark in the appropriate column to the right of each statement.

		T	?	F
01.	Members of my work group regularly use statistical methods to ensure methods to ensure product/service quality.	☐	☐	☐
02.	The average employee in my work group consistently meets the quality standards for his/her job.	☐	☐	☐
03.	I regularly involve the employees in my work group in solving problems that affect their work.	☐	☐	☐
04.	We regularly ask for employees' opinions and suggestions.	☐	☐	☐
05.	Our group works together effectively as a team.	☐	☐	☐
06.	Quality related information is shared among all of the employees in our work group who need it.	☐	☐	☐
07.	We regularly obtain information about the needs and expectations of our team's customers.	☐	☐	☐
08.	The employees in my work group are totally committed to meet all of our customers' needs.	☐	☐	☐
09.	My employees receive continuous education and job skill development.	☐	☐	☐
10.	My employees receive recognition and rewards for quality improvement.	☐	☐	☐

Personal Developmental Plan

Prepare a development plan to improve your TQM skills by answering the following questions.

A. The TQM skills that I use most frequently and that are currently my greatest strengths are:

B. The TQM skills in which I currently need the greatest improvement are:

C. My personal objectives for improving my TQM skills are:

D. The specific strategies by which I plan to develop and strengthen my TQM skills are (use additional paper if necessary):

   1.

   2.

   3.

   4.

   5.

Appendix A

Self-Awareness Test Answers

1. The Role And Responsibility Of A Leader

1. True

2. False. Effective managers are team builders and members of teams. Superior teams collaborate rather than compete.

3. False. Their main responsibility is to accomplish their work group's goals which include representing the interests of both management and the employees.

4. False. The most important skills for supervisors are the human skills - interacting effectively with others.

5. False. The human skills are as important for working supervisors as they are for other supervisors.

6. False. The term refers to the four basic functions of management.

7. True.

8. False. Leadership is basically a process of influence.

9. False. All supervisors have the responsibility to plan, organize, implement and ensure that their plans are carried out (control).

10. True. Directing is also called implementing.

2. Developing Leadership Skills

1. False. Leaders cannot lead unless followers agree to follow. Even the worst coercion can be rejected, albeit at the risk of serious consequence.

2. False. Leadership is follower acceptance and power of influence based.

3. False. The most effective leadership approach will vary with the task, the people and the situation.

4. False. The role of a supervisor may change but not his/her power.

5. True.

6. True.

7. True.

8. True.

9. True.

10. True.

3. Building A Winning Team

The Test is a measurement of the respondents' perceptions about their team leadership behaviors. The most successful team leaders will have answered **True** to all of the questions in this test.

4. Communicating And Active Listening

1. False. Communication is not limited to written and verbal forms. It also includes non-verbal forms. Further, communication requires both the sharing and processing of information (messages).

2. True.

3. False. It is only 25%.

4. False. These are often the least effective ways.

5. False. That responsibility is important, of course. However, the work group leader must ensure that there is an open and effective **two-way** channel of communication with employees about essential job related information. This means feedback from employees and upward communication between superiors and their superiors.

6. False. The "grapevine" and other informal channels are not the proper way to communicate with employees. An employee's immediate supervisor should be the authoritative, timely and accurate source of job related information for him or her.

7. True.

8. True..

9. True. Most people feel very uncomfortable when there is silence and feel compelled to say something.

10. True.

5. Motivating Through Empowerment

In order to have a valid empowerment initiative in your work group the response to all of the Test items in this chapter should be **True.**

6. Solving Problems Effectively

1. True.

2. False. Many, if not most, decisions do not deal with problems.

3. False. Studies have shown that the majority of managers and supervisors require further skill development in problem solving methods.

4. True.

5. False. The first step is to accurately identify the issue.

6. True.

7. False. The basic method is the same in either case. However, team problem solving also requires additional interaction skills.

8. False. Compromise does not solve the problem giving rise to conflict. It is a form of appeasement.

9. False. This is because the most effective conflict resolution method is problem solving.

10. False. Systematic methods can also be used to solve "people" problems.

7. Improving Planning Skills

1. False. Human and technical skills are required. However, planning requires mostly conceptual skills.

2. True. However, a sub-component of objective setting is anticipating a future event for which planning will be required.

3. True. This is a visionary skill which is the first step in setting an objective.

4. True.

5. False. Planning involves developing strategies. Organizing involves gathering resources.

6. True. One can perform unnecessary or low priority tasks efficiently. The key is to be effective.

7. False. The "ABC" system involves arranging tasks in three categories of importance or urgency.

8. False. The ultimate responsibility for task performance cannot be delegated

9. True.

10. True.

8. Training Employees To Succeed

1. False. Training subordinates is a key responsibility of all managers, supervisors and other work group leaders.

2. True. Effective trainers must be skilled in both verbal and non-verbal communication.

3. False. The term refers to a state when someone does not recognize his or her own knowledge or skill deficiency.

4. False. Demonstrations are far more effective than lectures. The latter are among the least effective methods.

5. False. Inter-cultural problems can arise at any time.

6. False. The employee must accept responsibility for his or her own actions. However, primary responsibility rests with the supervisor.

7. True. This is a greatly different role from past eras.

8. False. In many cultures a nod or silence is a way to minimize loss of face. In others it is simply a sign of attention or polite interest -- but not necessarily understanding.

9. False. It is the employee's background and experience that the supervisor must consider.

10. True.

9. Improving Employee Work Performance

1. False. The behavior and practices of an employee's immediate supervisor are crucial to the former's performance success; i.e. training, coaching, problem solving, etc.

2. True.

3. False. Standards can be established for almost all jobs.

4. True.

5. False. These elements also strongly affect motivation.

6. False. Performance appraisal has two **equally** important purposes: (1) to evaluate performance and (2) to develop performance capability and potential.

7. False. Among other benefits, performance standards help employees understand what is expected of them.

8. False. Discipline is usually not an effective way to improve skill (versus non- skill) deficiencies.

9. False. Discipline as a concept is positive, constructive and morale building. Only punitive discipline should be used sparingly.

10. True. Focusing on the record versus on the personal characteristics of the employee helps preserve the employee's dignity and sense of self worth.

10. Coaching And Counseling

1. False. Coaching and counseling do require the same skills. However, coaching is a confrontational activity that focuses on improving job performance. Counseling deals with employees complaints, concerns and other job related problems.

2. True.

3. False. See #1 above.

4. False. The absence of complaints could indicate that employees are fearful of speaking up.

5. False. Although coaching involves candidly confronting performance problems, its purpose is to improve performance and to develop job competencies.

6. True.

7. False. Small talk puts very few people at ease. You should begin by explaining the purpose and objectives of the meeting.

8. False. Most employees are both objective and honest.

9. True. Coaching is a neglected skill.

10. True. It increases the employee's commitment to the solution.

11. Managing Cultural Diversity

1. False. They are the fastest growing segment.

2. False. Accent and understanding are not necessarily related.

3. False. They can and often do differ considerably.

4. False. They can and often do vary considerably.

5. False. It is better to understand and respect cultural differences than to try to get people of other cultures to adopt American values.

6. False. Many cultures would not understand this approach.

7. False. Technology is only one of the many criteria by which the sophistication of a culture can be judged.

8. False. It is a low context culture.

9. False. Some place primary emphasis on the achievements of a group or team rather than on the individual.

10. False. About 60% is conveyed through non-verbal behavior.

12. Focusing On Total Quality

In this chapter the Test is actually a measurement of perceptions of the respondent rather than an objective test. Its purpose is to help the student focus on work group behaviors which are supportive of a total quality effort. In order to have a valid TQM work group initiative the response to **all** of the Test items should be **True.**

Appendix B

Dr. W. Edward Deming's 14 Points

Deming's 14 Points

1. Create constancy of purpose for improvement of product and service.//
2. Adopt this philosophy and aim to take on leadership change.
3. Do not depend 100% on inspection to improve quality levels.
4. Stop awarding business for price only.
5. Improve the system of production and service.
6. Institute training.
7. Adopt and institute leadership.
8. Drive out fear.
9. Break down and eliminate barriers.
10. Eliminate slogans and exhortations.
11. Eliminate numerical quotas for the work force.
12. Get rid of barriers that rob people of pride in what they do.
13. Encourage education and self-improvement for all.
14. Take action.

Appendix C

Leadership Skills Test

Leadership Skills Test

Developed by
Louis E. Tagliaferri, Ph.D.

Respondent Booklet
MD-127EPB

Leadership Skills Test

INSTRUCTIONS: Below are 40 pairs of behaviors and practices that might apply to the role of a leader in any organization. Read each pair of items carefully. Decide which one of each pair you believe is more characteristic than the other of the behavior or practice of a modern leader. Then circle the letter of that item (either "a" or "b") in the column to the left of the pair. In some cases you may believe that both behaviors or practices in a pair are equally characteristic of a modern leader while in other cases you may believe that neither is characteristic. If the former, select the statement that is most consistent with your beliefs. If the latter, select the statement that is least inconsistent with them.

01. a. Training employees in new skills.
    b. Resolving a conflict between two members of a team.

02. a. Helping employees identify work related problems and causes.
    b. Helping employees cope with problems that adversely affect their quality of life.

03. a. Helping employees solve problems beyond their skill level.
    b. Maintaining control over the tasks and work schedules of employees.

04. a. Analyzing the number and type of customer complaints.
    b. Obtaining feedback from customers about how well their needs were met.

05. a. Meeting with employees in a work unit to discuss how well they work together.
    b. Identifying which employees in a group are the potential trouble makers.

06. a. Involving employees in making decisions that affect them.
    b. Ensuring that decisions are made by only the most qualified people.

07. a. Sticking to envisioned objectives even when the unpredicted occurs.
    b. Changing objectives when the unpredicted occurs.

08. a. Beginning the first phase of a project by organizing the necessary resources.
    b. Making sure that the project team is trained in all required skills.

09. a. Finding ways to help employees reach their goals and succeed.
    b. Setting realistic goals for your own personal success.

10. a. Asking employees to identify activities that will be hurt by a planned change.
    b. Preparing employees for possible future unplanned changes.

11. a. Checking to see if an employee is following instructions.
    b. Listening to an employee who is complaining about a work assignment.

12. a. Being willing and available to make the necessary decisions.
    b. Authorizing employees to make as many decisions as possible by themselves.

13. a. Knowing who the "customers" are within the organization.
    b. Knowing how the organization's products or services are used.

14. a. Designing a compensation plan that will effectively motivate employees.
    b. Developing an employee's commitment to the process of continual learning.

15. a. Asking for information that will explain the reasons for a planned change.
    b. Offering constructive criticism about planned changes that don't make sense.

16. a. Sharing rewards for success with all members of the team.
    b. Allocating rewards to the most deserving members of the team.

17. a. Having employees solve their own work related problems.
    b. Encouraging employees to discuss their work related problems with you.

18. a. Finding creative solutions to problems.
    b. Making sure that there are no problems.

19. a. Eliminating anything that prevents being able to predict an outcome.
    b. Maintaining a sense of control during periods of uncertainty.

20. a. Making employees understand their responsibility for meeting team goals.
    b. Taking personal responsibility for the team's failure to meet its goals.

21. a. Allocating most of the time to develop a solution to the problem.
    b. Allocating most of the time to identifying the problem and its causes.

22. a. Trying to solve persistent technical problems.
    b. Advising employees how to become more sensitive to the organization culture.

23. a. Determining what issues have to be decided in a particular problem.
    b. Determining who caused the problem and why it exists.

24. a. Establishing a relaxed atmosphere to encourage optimum team performance.
    b. Helping work teams stay focused on meeting performance goals.

25. a. Showing employees in a work unit how to critique their team effectiveness.
    b. Establishing controls to maintain work group discipline and morale.

26. a. Explaining work rules to employees.
    b. Keeping employees informed about work related matters that affect them.

27. a. Encouraging friendly competition between the employees of two work groups.
    b. Encouraging employees to work together on a project.

28. a. Deciding which employees have the best skills to solve a work group problem.
    b. Involving all employees in a work group to solve a problem affecting them.

29. a. Responding promptly and effectively to customer complaints.
    b. Developing strategies to deal with difficult customers.

30. a. Developing a fair reward system for ideas and suggestions.
    b. Making sure that employees receive credit for their ideas.

31. a. Using SPC and other statistical methods to develop project schedules.
    b. Developing control methods to ensure that the project plan is being followed.

32. a. Producing a product or service of the highest possible quality.
    b. Being committed to meeting all of the customer's expectations.

33. a. Holding a meeting to find out what caused a production problem.
    b. Holding a meeting to obtain employees' suggestions to reduce waste.

34. a. Helping employees find a way to resolve interpersonal conflicts.
    b. Establishing standards for employee conduct and behavior.

35. a. Ensuring that employees arrive at work on time.
    b. Ensuring that employees have the resources they need to do their jobs properly.

36. a. Helping to develop the skills and abilities of project team members.
    b. Replacing unproductive project team members with other employees.

37. a. Helping work teams accomplish their tasks more effectively.
    b. Working on a plan to improve personal time management.

38. a. Completing weekly reports to management about work unit performance.
    b. Ensuring that employees have information they need to do their jobs properly.

39. a. Anticipating future events and planning how to deal with them.
    b. Dealing on a practical level with the problems of today.

40. a. Comparing an employee's actual performance with performance standards.
    b. Deciding what an employee must do to improve job performance.

LEADERSHIP SKILLS CHART

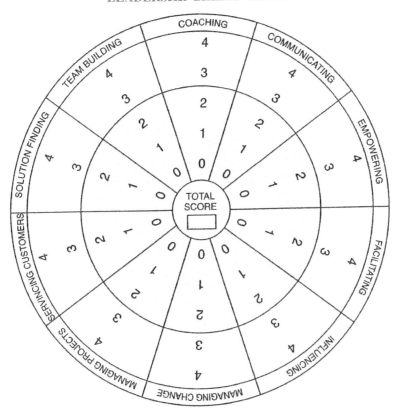

INSTRUCTIONS: The answers for the Leadership Skills Test are on the next page of this guide. Circle the number of items that you answered correctly in each dimension of the above Leadership Skills Chart. Circled numbers that fall within the shaded section (0, 1, or 2) indicate that you may have a development need in that particular leadership skill dimension. Next, write the total of correct answers both in the Total Score box and also in the congruence scale that is found immediately below the chart. This score shows the extent that your overall leadership behaviors and practices are congruent with those required of leaders in today's work force and also the extent that you may have an overall leadership skill development need.

Low	Congruence with Effective Leadership Behavior	High
0 • • • • • • • • • 10 • • • • • • • • • 20 • • • • • • • • • 30 • • • • • • • • • 40		
High	Leadership Development Need	Low

Test Answers and Skill Dimensions

Below is a list of the leadership skill dimensions that the LST evaluates. The numbers in parenthesis indicate those answers which are most congruent with modern leadership behavior and practices.

Coaching: (02a) (14b) (22b) (40a)

Improving the competencies and commitment of employees through a process of coaching that employs the functions of counseling, mentoring, tutoring and confronting with respect to problems and situations that can affect their job performance.

Communicating: (11b) (26b) (33b) (38b)

Establishing and maintaining open, two-way communication with employees that provides them with essential job related information and obtains feedback about their problems, concerns and suggestions.

Empowering: (06a) (12b) (16a) (20a)

Developing the competencies and influence of employees, both as individuals and as teams of individuals, in a way that involves shared responsibility, shared rewards and a focus on meeting performance objectives.

Facilitating: (25a) (34a) (35b) (37a)

Intervening in the work activities of employees for the purpose of helping them to increase their full performance potential, to solve work related problems and to achieve their performance objectives. Strengthening employees by providing resources, clarifying roles and norms and helping them develop effective work processes.

Influencing: (03a) (09a) (17b) (30b)

Achieving leader acceptance and willing followers by using the process of influence based on the power of expertise and referent power, by inspiring and by creating challenging, achievable goals for employees.

Managing Change: (07a) (10b) (15a) (19b)

Being an effective agent for change by focusing on goal attainment and maintaining a sense of control during periods of uncertainty while at the same time demonstrating flexibility and adaptability. Preparing employees to respond to change constructively.

Managing Projects: (08b) (31b) (36a) (39a)

Envisioning future events and developing strategies for dealing with them. Being able to develop project plans, train and develop project team skills and establish and follow appropriate project control measures to ensure goal attainment.

Servicing Customers: (04b) (13a) (29a) (32b)

Providing quality service to both internal and external customers. Committing oneself and one's team to meeting all of the customer's needs and expectations. Using customer feedback for purposes of continuous improvement.

Solution Finding: (18a) (21b) (23a) (28b)

Defining the problem and understanding the real problem or decision issue. Effectively using both creative and rational problem solving skills in a way that assures full inclusion of all members of the team.

Team Building: (01a) (05a) (24b) (27b)

Accomplishing performance objectives through effective teamwork. Building teams by training employees in team skills, encouraging team interaction and by facilitating team development through open feedback and constructive critique.

150

References

Anderson, Terry D., Transforming Leadership: New Skills for an Extraordinary Future, HRD Press, Inc., Amherst, MA, 1992.

Axelrod, Alan, Patton on Leadership: Strategic Lessons for Corporate Warfare, Paramus, NJ, Prentice Hall Press, 1999.

Hersey, Paul, Blanchard, Kenneth H, and Johnson, Dewey E., Management of Organizational Behavior (9th Edition), Paramus, NJ, Prentice Hall Press, 2007.

Kaltman, Al, Cigars, Whiskey & Winning Leadership Lessons, Paramus, NJ, Prentice Hall Press, 1998.

Kinlaw, Dennis C., Developing Superior Work Teams, University Associates, Inc., San Diego, CA, 1991.

Kirkpatrick, Donald L., How to Train and Develop Supervisors, Amacom, New York, 1993.

Lefton, Robert E. and Buzzotta, Victor R, Leadership Through People Skills, New York, 2004.

Tagliaferri, Louis E., How to Achieve Superior Teamwork, Ponte Vedra Beach, FL, Talico Developmental Systems L.C., 2010.

Tagliaferri, Louis E., Successful Supervision, NY, John Wiley & Sons, Inc., 1979.

Thiederman, Sondra, Bridging Cultural Barriers for Corporate Success, New York, Lexington Books, 1991.

Tjosvold, Dean W. And Tjosvold, Mary M., Leading the Team Organization, New York, Lexington Books, 1991.

Zenger, John H., Not Just for CEOs, Sure-Fire Success Secrets for the Leaders in Each of Us, Richard D. Irwin, Chicago, 1996.